W9-BFP-668

COLLABORATIONS:
ENGLISH IN OUR LIVES

Literacy Worktext

The publication of *Collaborations* was directed by the members of the Heinle & Heinle Secondary and Adult ESL Publishing Team:

Editorial Director: Roseanne Mendoza
Senior Production Services Coordinator: Lisa McLaughlin
Market Development Director: Andy Martin

Also participating in the publication of the program were:

Vice President and Publisher ESL: Stanley Galek
Senior Assistant Editor: Sally Conover
Production Editor: Maryellen Killeen
Manufacturing Coordinator: Mary Beth Hennebury
Full Service Design and Production: PC&F, Inc.
Illustration Program: G. Brian Karas and PC&F, Inc.

Manufactured in the United States of America.

ISBN: 0-8384-6624-9

Heinle & Heinle is a division of International Thomson Publishing, Inc.

Photo Credits

Cover: Thai-Hung Pham Nguyen, top; Marie H. Bias, center left; David Moss, center middle and bottom; Betty Lynch, center right.

Unit 1: Mark Neyndorff, 1, 2; David Moss, 6 top, bottom right, 7 top left, 19; Greater Corpus Christi Business Alliance, 6 bottom; Thai-Hung Pham Nguyen, 7 bottom right; Jeanne H. Schmedlen, 13; © Jonathan Stark/Heinle & Heinle Publishers, 8, 18.

Unit 2: Sarah Hoskins, 21, 22; David Moss, 26, 27, 30, 31, 33.

Unit 3: James Higgins, 39, 40; Anne Nafziger, 44 top; David Moss, 44 bottom, 45 bottom, 50; Thai-Hung Pham Nguyen, 45 top; Ziglang Shr, 47 left; Jann Huizenga, 47 right, 50, 51.

Unit 4: David Moss, 64, 65 bottom; © Jonathan Stark/Heinle & Heinle Publishers, 65 top and middle; Marie H. Bias, 69.

Unit 5: Jann Huizenga, 77, 78; David Moss, 83, 86, 87, 88, 91; Donna Moss, 86 bottom left.

Unit 6: Peter Lee, 95, 96; © Jonathan Stark/Heinle & Heinle Publishers, 100, 102, 105 bottom; Marie H. Bias, 103, 110, 112; David Moss, 104 bottom; Thai-Hung Nguyen, 104 top, 105 top, middle; Henry Schmedlen, 113.

Practice Pages: Harry Bornstein, Karen L. Sauinier, and Lillian B. Hamilton, editors, signs from *The Comprehensive Signed English Dictionary,* 1983. Washington, DC: Gallaudet University Press. Copyright © 1983 Gallaudet University. Reprinted by permission, 124; David Moss, 130, 132.

Cut-out Pages: David Moss, money photos.

COLLABORATIONS:
ENGLISH IN OUR LIVES

Literacy Worktext

Donna Moss
Cathy C. Shank
Lynda Terrill

This *Literacy Worktext* is designed to be used in literacy level classes and also in mixed classes that have both low beginning and literacy students. For this reason, the *Literacy Worktext* follows the thematic development as *Collaborations Beginning 1*, begins with the same story and photos, and simplifies and adapts many *Beginning 1* activities. The development of the worktext would not have been possible without the creativity and pioneering efforts of *Collaborations Beginning 1* authors Jann Huizenga and Gail Weinstein-Shr, whose work provided the central framework for the book.

Heinle & Heinle Publishers
A Division of International Thomson Publishing, Inc.
Boston, MA 02116, U.S.A.

I T P   The ITP logo is a trademark under license.

CONTENTS

Basic Skills	Higher Order Skills and Strategies	Community Building in the Classroom
• saying, writing alphabet • matching capital and small letters • saying, reading, writing country • writing letters from dictation • recognizing new vocabulary in context	• finding one's country on a map • sequencing events chronologically • evaluating one's learning	• locating our countries on a map • telling our stories with timelines
• saying, writing numbers • saying, writing telephone numbers • writing numbers from dictation • writing birthdate • recognizing new vocabulary in context	• thinking about learning preferences • sequencing events chronologically • evaluating one's learning	• getting help from classmates • sharing ways we learn • telling our stories with timelines
• saying, reading, writing address • recognizing new vocabulary in context • writing birthplace	• problem solving for homesickness • sequencing events chronologically • classifying by gender • evaluating one's learning	• learning about one another's family • sharing family photos • telling our stories with timelines
• reading, writing time • matching digital time to analog time • saying, reading days of the week • recognizing new vocabulary in context	• plotting out weekly schedules • comparing daily schedules • comparing jobs and housework • sequencing events chronologically • evaluating one's learning	• sharing daily schedules • telling our stories with timelines
• identifying coins, bills by name and value • reading, writing prices • producing requested amounts • recognizing new vocabulary in context	• solving problems • comparing prices • problem solving for places to meet people • sequencing events chronologically • evaluating one's learning	• sharing ideas on places to meet people • telling our stories with timelines
• reading, writing dates • matching abbreviated form to full form: months, days • using a calendar to locate dates • recognizing new vocabulary in context	• comparing holidays and celebrations • listing traditions to keep or change • sequencing events chronologically • evaluating one's learning	• sharing favorite celebrations • planning a party • telling about things we miss from our country • telling our stories with timelines

THE WORLD

Do you want to see where the people in this book come from? Their countries are labeled.

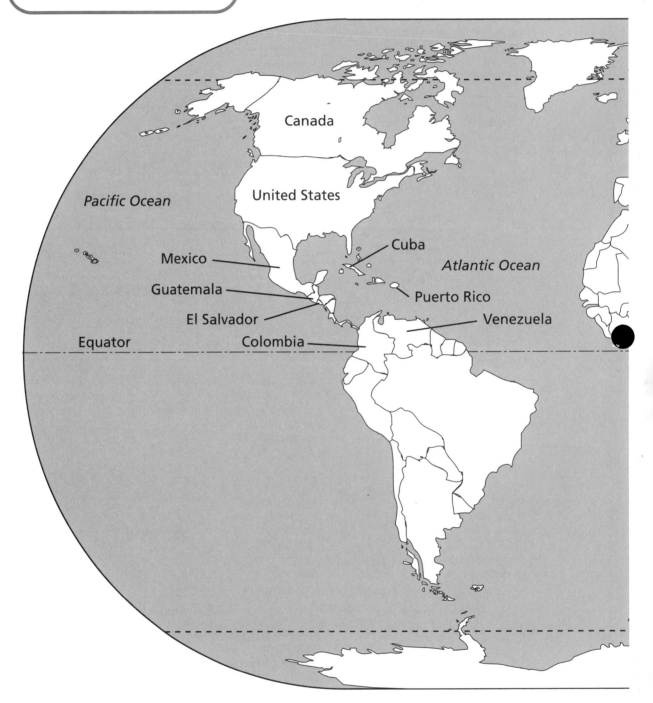

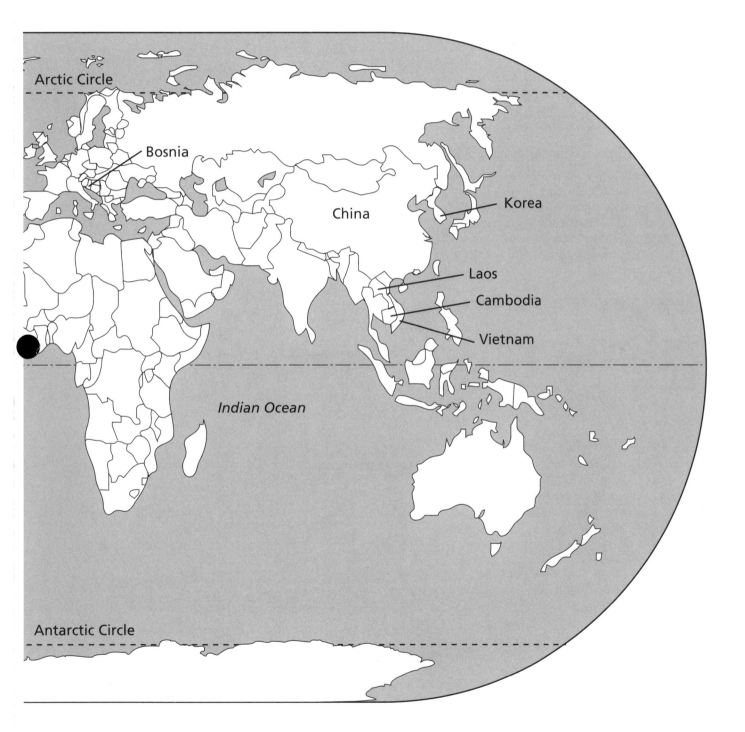

Arctic Circle

Bosnia

China

Korea

Laos

Cambodia

Vietnam

Indian Ocean

Antarctic Circle

ABOUT THIS SERIES

Our purpose for creating this series is to provide opportunities for adult immigrants and refugees to develop English language and literacy skills while reflecting, as individuals and with others, on their changing lives.

We believe that the best adult ESL classrooms are places where learners and teachers work collaboratively, talk about issues that matter to them, use compelling materials, and engage in tasks that reflect their life experiences and concerns. We see learning as a process in which students are encouraged to participate actively, and the classroom as a place where students share and reflect on their experiences and rehearse for new roles in the English-speaking world beyond its walls.

How are the books in the series organized?

Unlike most adult ESL materials, *Collaborations* is not organized around linguistic skills nor life skills competencies, but around contexts for language use in learners' lives. Each student book consists of six units, beginning with the individual and moving out through the series of ever-widening language environments shown below.

```
6   Global Community
  5   Local Community
    4    Work
      3   Home
        2 School
         1 Self
```

The units revolve around the narratives of newcomers who tell or write of their experiences. It is our belief that within the marvelous diversity of newcomers, there are seeds for finding similarities—the common threads of experience—as newcomers make sense of managing life in a new setting with new constraints as well as new possibilities.

Grammar, vocabulary development, language functions, and competencies are interwoven throughout the units in each student book. However, the organizing principles are reversed from those of most traditional materials. Rather than selecting linguistic items and then creating contexts to elicit them, *Collaborations* addresses language development and competencies as they naturally emerge from the contexts and the authentic texts. For those who wish to focus more on specific competencies or language structures, detailed indexes are provided to enable participants to identify where the item is taught, with resources for further practice in the teacher's materials.

ABOUT THIS WORKTEXT

What activities are included in each unit?

• The opening *Story* is an opportunity to look at a photo while listening to a simple authentic narrative (based on photos, student writings, interview material) collected from newcomers throughout the United States and Canada.
• *Play with the Story* gives learners practice in reading and copying the story, completing cloze and comprehension activities, and responding to the story in a personal way.
• Each *Picture Dictionary* introduces new words related to the unit and gives learners the chance to identify and write additional vocabulary on the same topic.
• Two pages of *Photos* stimulate discussion and critical thinking while reinforcing new words and developing additional key vocabulary and concepts.
• *My Teacher* allows learners to hear authentic and natural language from their best source of input— their teacher.
• A second authentic *Story* with an accompanying photo, gives additional comprehension tasks and encourages learners to think and write about themselves.
• The *Timeline* for each unit encourages learners to gather data about one individual's life and develop their own timelines to tell their own life stories.
• Each *Picture Story* initiates a discussion on a familiar theme while providing practice in interpreting pictures and retelling a story sequentially.
• *Ideas for Action* is a chance for learners to reflect critically on their situations and what they can do to act on them.
• *Looking Back* provides learners an opportunity to monitor their own progress, review previous materials, and indicate which learning activities suit them the most.
• *Practice Activities* at the back of the book introduce or reinforce very basic literacy and numeracy skills for those who need the practice.
• *Cut-out Activities* at the back of the book provide hands-on reinforcement of basic concepts and skills and are used in conjunction with listening activities on the cassette tape.

What are other features of *Collaborations Literacy Level?*

The *teacher's materials* for the literacy level are designed to extend classroom activities and to facilitate and to assess learners' progress. The materials listed below are provided in a format that can be inserted into a binder.
• the teacher's edition
• blackline activity masters

© 1997 Heinle & Heinle Publishers

- overhead transparencies
- the cassette tape
- the assessment program
- wall maps of the world and of North America

The **teacher's edition** includes reduced student book pages, suggestions from the authors, insights from field test instructors who used the material in their classes, and space for teachers to keep their own teaching/learning journals.

The **activity masters** complement the worktext by providing additional practice in each of the skill areas. In order to address the multilevel nature of literacy groups, reading/writing activity masters are provided at both an A (lower literacy) and B (higher literacy) level. They are designed so that learners at different levels can be engaged in the same type of task in the same classroom as they work at different levels of literacy.

The **transparencies** can be used for whole group pre-reading, problem-posing activities, Language Experience writing, and oral language practice.

The **cassette tape** contains the stories (including the picture story) from each unit of the worktext as well as listening exercises to accompany both the cut-out activity pages at the end of the worktext and the listening activities found in the activity masters.

The **assessment program** includes an instrument to assist in choosing appropriate literacy materials. It also includes an array of intake, initial, on-going, and final assessment instruments, as well as guidelines for developing learner portfolios.

The *worktext* along with the *teacher's materials* provide a full course for literacy learners. In many programs, literacy and low beginning level learners are often placed in the same classroom. *Collaborations* materials can make it possible for teachers to work with both groups of learners together in the same classroom.

How can I work with Literacy and Beginning 1 learners in the same classroom?

The *Collaborations* series is unique in using the *Literacy Worktext* and the *Beginning 1* materials together in a multilevel classroom that fosters easy interaction between the groups. At the outset of each unit, whole class pre-reading discussions and listening activities are possible because the first activity at both *Collaborations* levels features the same photo and personal story. At the literacy level, the amount of text and the degree of difficulty is significantly reduced. Throughout each unit, interactive listening and speaking activities are also designed to include both groups.

While the two *Collaborations* levels are designed to follow the same themes, in much the same sequence, activities in the latter part of each unit are distinctly different. The *Literacy Worktext*

offers a different second story followed by comprehension activities and guided writing practice. The two-page photo spread, picture story, and timeline activities are also unique to the literacy level.

UNDERLYING PRINCIPLES

In a multilevel literacy class, will all the learners be able to successfully use the worktext and understand the materials?

In our experience, even a "pure" *literacy level* group is usually a *multilevel* group both in terms of written skills and spoken language. A literacy class may include: adults with little or no exposure to written language of any kind as well as those who have had some primary schooling in another language. In addition, some adults enter a literacy group even though they have a background of education in another language. These adults may be unaccustomed to using our alphabetic system of writing or they simply require a slower-paced, multi-sensory approach to learning a new language.

Adult learners with limited skills in English literacy may have no such limitations in understanding or speaking the language. As with other adult ESL learners, this group exhibits a continuum of listening and speaking skills (from almost no ability to communicate to a moderate amount of fluency).

The *Literacy Worktext* exposes literacy level learners to a broad range of listening and speaking opportunities while taking into consideration the need for extra practice and reinforcement in the areas of reading and writing. The *worktext* includes activities that will provide appropriate practice for learners beginning to read and write for the first time as well as those who simply need extra time to process written language.

Will my students get enough practice in basic skills?

Literacy learners with very limited previous experience with either print or spoken English need to go at a very slow pace with a great deal of reinforcement. If a native language literacy class is available, we believe these learners should be encouraged to also attend such a program.

The *worktext* and *teacher's materials* offer exposure to vocabulary and concepts in a larger group setting. They also provide drill and practice with flash cards and manipulatives; the opportunity to pronounce and copy letters, numerals, and new words; and the chance to discuss and illustrate new ideas. Some learners may remain in an English literacy group for a long period of time. Recycling stories and some activities as they repeat the same level will add to their grasp of new concepts and vocabulary. Selecting different activities from the *teacher's materials* will offer new opportunities to expand their skills.

Learners who have had some previous exposure to print and to spoken English, may not require an introduction to letters, numerals, and words but rather may need extensive practice to refine literacy skills. The *worktext* offers opportunities to label new words, read simple stories, sequence picture stories, develop Language Experience stories and even do controlled writing about themselves. The *teacher's materials* offer *A-level* activities to reinforce new vocabulary, skills, and concepts.

Adults who are conversant in the English language but struggle with print language often require some transition to a regular ESL classroom. For these learners, the *worktext* provides the opportunity to focus on basic skills practice while using and improving the full range of their speaking abilities. The *teacher's materials* provide *B-level* activities to expand their skills.

What do I do if my students do not yet know the grammar or vocabulary in the stories and tasks?

Any teacher who has ever faced a class of eager ESL learners has had to grapple with the reality that learners come with differences in their prior exposure to English and with their own individual language learning timetables, strategies, and abilities. There is no syllabus that will address directly and perfectly the stage of language development of any particular learner, let alone a diverse group. This material reflects the belief that learners can benefit most when forms and functions are made available in the service of authentic communicative tasks. Teaching is most effective when it taps into areas that are ready for development.

For this reason, tasks in *Collaborations* are open-ended and multi-faceted, allowing individuals to make progress according to their current stages of development. The inclusion of numerous collaborative tasks makes it possible for more capable peers as well as instructors to provide assistance to learners as they move to new stages of growth in mastering English.

It is not necessary for learners to understand every word or grammatical structure in order to respond to a story, theme, or issue. The context created by evocative photographs, by familiar situations, and by predicable tasks usually allows learners to make good guesses about meaning even when they do not control all of the vocabulary or structures they see. Any given reading or activity is suc-

cessful if it evokes a reaction in the learner, and if it creates a situation in which learners are eager to respond. When appropriate language structures and vocabulary are provided toward that end, language acquisition is facilitated. Within this framework, total mastery is not critical: total engagement is.

ACKNOWLEDGMENTS

We would like to thank those individuals whose stories are at the heart of this work. Their names appear after each story. We are grateful to colleagues, teachers, and administrators who helped so much in arranging interviews and photos, and collecting stories, among them Michael Westover and Judy Sides (Immigration and Refugee Services of Catholic Charities of Harrisburg, PA); The Partners (Jubilee Partners, Comer, GA); Cheryl Rowan and Karen Kern (Kanawha County Schools/RESA III Adult Basic Education Program, WV); Inaam Mansoor, (Arlington Education Employment Program—REEP, VA); Jean Rose, Susanna Levitt, and Bob Marseille (ABC School, Cerritos, CA); Jenny Witner (Chicago Commons, IL); Harriet Lindenburg (Santa Fe Community College, NM) Marta Pitts (Lindsey Hopkins Technical Education Center, Miami, FL); Leann Howard and Eileen Schmitz (San Diego Community College, CA).

We thank the many fine photographers whose work is included here, and especially those whose work appears repeatedly: David Moss, without whom this book could not have been accomplished, Thai-Hung Pham Nguyen, Marie H. Bias, Jann Huizenga, and James Higgins.

We thank the many reviewers whose collective input has enriched our final product. Our field testers not only provided feedback but also allowed us to quote them extensively in the Teacher's Edition.

At Heinle & Heinle, we are grateful to *Collaborations* author Jean Bernard for wise insights and advice; to Editorial Director Roseanne Mendoza for including us in this challenging undertaking; to Sally Conover, assistant editor, for helping to resolve numerous publishing issues; to Lisa McLaughlin, production editor; and to Louise Gelinas and the staff at PC&F for their editing and production work.

We are all grateful to Miriam Burt at NCLE for making connections for us. We also thank our friends, colleagues, and students at REEP for their encouragement, inspiration, and support.

Donna would like to thank Robbie Buller, Chou Ly, the partners, volunteers, and refugees for their hospitality at Jubilee and Vlasta Zhang for her assistance as a translator. She also thanks her daughters for their good humor and understanding. Last, but never least, she thanks her husband David for his love, help, and great meals. Not only did he have his eye behind the camera for many of the book's pictures, but he kept a caring eye on her.

Cathy would like to thank her husband, Steve, for his ideas, reactions, and continual support, and Andy and Emily for patience with their mother.

Lynda thanks Jeanne and Dan for everything in Harrisburg, and her family for making room for the project. She also thanks her parents, Audrey and Hank, who knew the old stories and shared them with her.

Unit

 Linh's Story

Listen.

Linh Dang is from Vietnam.
She studies in San Diego, California.

Play with the Story

A. Listen and **read.**

> My name is Linh Dang.
> I am from Vietnam.
> I am single.
> I don't have children.

B. Copy the story.

_____

_____

_____

_____

C. Say the words in the box. **(Circle)** the words in the story above.

name	from	children	single

D. Write the missing words.

My _____ *name* _____ is Linh Dang.

I am _____ Vietnam.

I am _____ .

I don't have _____ .

E. (Circle) Yes or No.

    1. Her name is Linh Dang.   (Yes)   No

    2. She is from Virginia.   Yes   No

    3. She is single.   Yes   No

    4. She doesn't have children.   Yes   No

 F. Check your answers with the class.

G. Think about yourself.

> My name is _____.
>
> I am from _____.

H. Draw a picture of yourself.

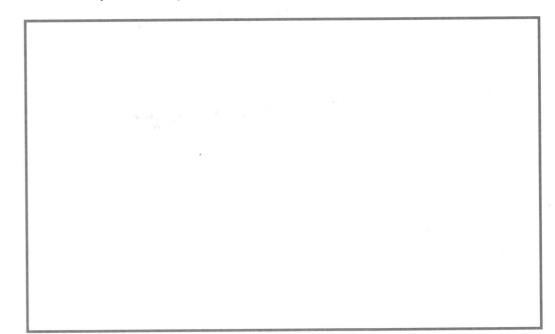

Countries

A. **Find** and **label** the United States.
   Find and **label** Canada.

B. **Find** and **label** your country.
   Color your country.

4 The World

A. **Look** at the pictures.
   What do you see?

B. **Look** at the words.
   Label the pictures.

city
temple
market
beach
mountains

mountains

_____

_____

C. Label other things you see.

D. Show a partner.

5 Your Country

A. Bring in pictures of your country.

B. Tell about your country.

My Teacher

single   married

A. Copy the words.

single _s i n g l e_ _____

married __ __ __ __ __ __ __   _married_ _____

B. Listen to your teacher.
   Copy the information.

Name:	
Country:	
Single or Married:	
Children:	

I have children.   I don't have children.

C. Copy the words.

have __ __ __ __   _____

don't have __ __ __ __   __ __ __ __

_____

D. Write about yourself.

| **Name:** |
| My name is _____. |
| **Country:** |
| I am from _____. |
| **Single or Married:** |
| I am _____. |
| **Children:** |
| I _____ children. |

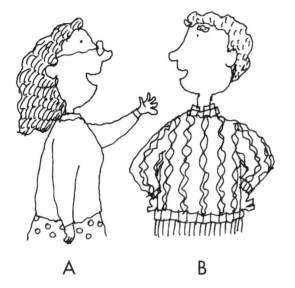

A   B

A: Are you single or married?

B: I am married.

A: Do you have children?

B: No, I don't have children.

Questions:

> What is your name?
> Where are you from?
> Are you single or married?
> Do you have children?

 A. Listen to your partner.
      Write the information.

Name:	_____
Country:	_____
Single or Married:	_____
Children:	_____

B. Listen. **Use** the alphabet cards.

C. Practice the alphabet on pages 120–124.

D. Listen and (circle) the letter.

1.	A	(E)	H
2.	F	H	S
3.	J	G	Z
4.	B	D	C
5.	O	R	L
6.	z	m	g
7.	c	s	z
8.	b	d	e
9.	g	c	j
10.	a	e	i

M-A-R-I-O

E. Spell and **write.**

your name _____

your country _____

A: What is your name?

B: My name is Jose Gomez.

A: Spell it, please.

B: J-o-s-e G-o-m-e-z

A: Where are you from?

B: I am from Cuba.

A: Spell it, please.

B: C-u-b-a

A   B

F. Ask the questions.
Write the answers.

Name	Country

Adriana's Story

A. Listen.

New Words

 B. Listen and **read.**

My name is Adriana Ariza.
I am from Colombia.
I am married.
My husband is from Puerto Rico.
I like to study.

C. (Circle) the words you know in the story.
Write new words in the box.

D. Read the story again. (Circle) Yes or No.

1. Her name is Adriana Ariza.	Yes	No
2. She is from Colombia.	Yes	No
3. She is single.	Yes	No
4. She is married.	Yes	No
5. Her husband is from Colombia.	Yes	No
6. She likes to study.	Yes	No

E. Check your answers with the class.

F. Think about yourself.
  (Circle) Yes or No.

I am from Colombia.	Yes	No
I am married.	Yes	No
I am single.	Yes	No
I have children.	Yes	No
I don't have children.	Yes	No
I like to study.	Yes	No
I don't like to study.	Yes	No

G. Copy your *Yes* sentences.

_____

_____

_____

_____

_____

_____

 **H. Show** a partner.

9 Things I Like to Do

I like to play soccer

I like to cook

A. Copy the words.

PICTURE DICTIONARY

cook _____ cook _____

dance _____

fish _____

play soccer _____ _____

shop _____

sleep _____

watch TV _____ _____

© 1997 Heinle & Heinle Publishers

••• 15

B. Make your own picture dictionary.
   Find pictures or **draw** pictures of things you like to do.

C. Write about things you like to do.

I like to _____.

and I like to _____.

D. Tell the class about things you like to do.

⦿10 Picture Story: Faduma

A. Look at the pictures. What do you see?

1. [Picture: Faduma in front of a world map, holding a suitcase labeled "U.S.A. Here I Come!"]

2. [Picture: Faduma sitting in a chair by a window, crying, holding a paper]

3. [Picture: A school building with a door. Sign reads "SCHOOL" and "Come to School — Learn English". Faduma standing outside with a bag.]

4. [Picture: A classroom with a teacher pointing at a board, students seated, and a "Welcome!" sign on the door. Faduma entering.]

B. Listen to the story.

C. Tell the story to a partner.

Faduma misses her country.

She is homesick.

She cries.

What can she do?

A. Talk about the problem.
Copy an idea.

_____

_____

_____

_____

B. Draw a picture of your idea.

12 Timeline

A. Look at the timeline.
Listen to Adela's story.

1967 — *I was born in La Union, El Salvador.*

1988 — *I came to the U.S. I lived in Washington, D.C.*

My name is Adela Flores. I live in Miami, Florida.

1986 — *I was married.*

B. Make pictures of your life.

C. Show the class your timeline.

Looking Back

Checklist for Learning

Check (✔) the words you know.

_____ read	_____ name	_____ cook
_____ listen	_____ country	_____ dance
_____ copy	_____ children	_____ fish
_____ think	_____ single	_____ shop
_____ tell	_____ married	_____ _____
_____ write	_____ like	_____ _____
_____ draw	_____ _____	_____ _____

Check (✔) what you can do.

_____ read stories	_____ say my name
_____ write the alphabet	_____ spell my name
_____ write my name	_____ tell about my life
_____ write about myself	

Write the page numbers.

I liked pages _____.

I did not like pages _____.

© 1997 Heinle & Heinle Publishers

 1 Alicia's Story

Listen.

Alicia Silva

Alicia Silva is from Guatemala.
She lives in Chicago, Illinois.

Play with the Story

A. Listen and **read.**

Alicia Silva

I like to read and write.
But I'm nervous because I don't speak.
I need more help.

B. Copy the story.

_____

_____

_____

_____

C. Say the words in the box. **Circle** the words in the story above.

read	write	speak	help

D. Write the missing words.

I like to _____ read _____ and _____.

But I'm nervous because I don't _____.

I need more _____.

E. (Circle) Yes or No.

    1. Alicia is from Bolivia   Yes   (No)

    2. Alicia likes to read.   Yes   No

    3. Alicia likes to speak.   Yes   No

    4. Alicia needs help.   Yes   No

 F. Check your answers with the class.

G. Think about yourself. (Circle) Yes or No.

Do you need help in English?   Yes   No

 # Ways I Like to Learn

A. (Circle) ways you like to learn.

speak	listen	speak my language
read	write	laugh
work alone	work with a partner	work with a group

 B. Tell your answers to a partner.

4 My Teacher

A. Listen to your teacher.

always   often   sometimes   never

B. (Circle) the things your teacher wants you to do.
    Check (✔) the things your teacher sometimes wants you to do.

speak	listen
speak my language	read
write	laugh
work alone	work with a partner
work with a group	

 **My Partner**

I am relaxed.

I am nervous.

 **A. Ask** your partner questions.

A

B

A: When are you nervous?

B: Speaking English.

A: When are you relaxed?

B: Reading.

B. Circle your partner's answers.

	Listening to English	Relaxed	Nervous
	Speaking English	Relaxed	Nervous
	Writing English	Relaxed	Nervous
	Reading English	Relaxed	Nervous

 **Ways to Learn**

A. Look at the pictures. What do you see?

B. Look at the words.
   Label the pictures.

listening
speaking
reading
writing

listening

© 1997 Heinle & Heinle Publishers

26 •••

C. Label other things you see.

 **D. Show** a partner.

7 In the Classroom

A. Copy the words.

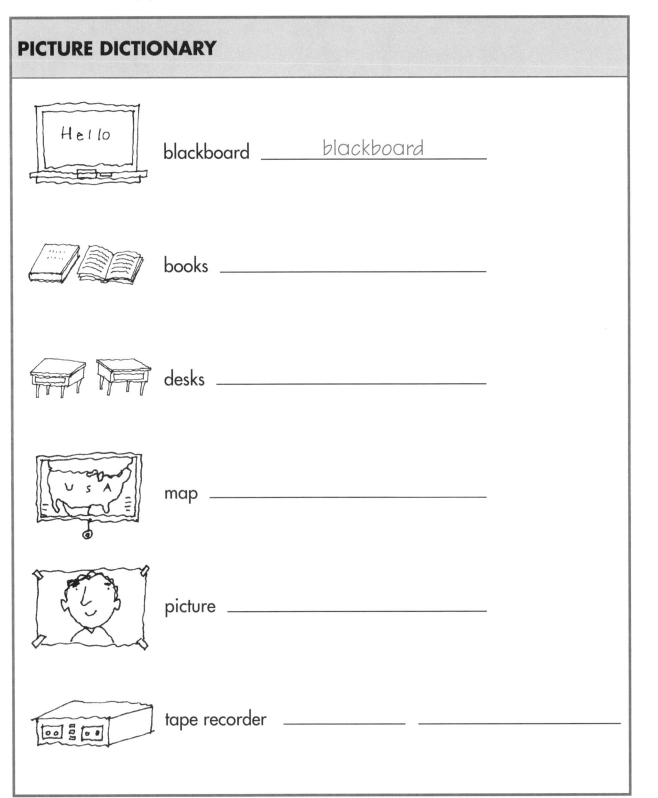

PICTURE DICTIONARY

blackboard   _blackboard_ _____

books _____

desks _____

map _____

picture _____

tape recorder _____ _____

© 1997 Heinle & Heinle Publishers

28 •••

B. Make your own Picture Dictionary.
   Find pictures or **draw** pictures of things in your classroom.

C. Look at the picture.
What do you see?

D. Look at the words.
Label the picture.

> blackboard
> books
> desks
> map
> picture
> tape recorder

tape recorder

E. Label other things you see.

F. Show a partner.

Mesud's Story

A. Listen.

Mesud Softic is from Bosnia.
He lives in Atlanta, Georgia.

B. Listen and read.

I study English at home.

I have pictures with words.

I look at the pictures.

I read the words.

I say the words.

The pictures help me learn.

New Words

C. Circle the words you know in the story.
Write new words in the box.

D. Read the story again. (**Circle**) Yes or No

1. Mesud studies at school.   Yes   (No)
2. Mesud studies at home.   Yes   No
3. The pictures help Mesud learn.   Yes   No
4. He looks at the blackboard.   Yes   No
5. He reads the words.   Yes   No

E. Check your answers with the class.

F. Think about yourself. (**Circle**) Yes or No.

I study at school.	Yes	No
I study at home.	Yes	No
I look at pictures.	Yes	No
I read words.	Yes	No
I say the words.	Yes	No
Pictures help me learn.	Yes	No

G. Copy your *Yes* sentences

_____

_____

_____

_____

_____

9 Things that Help Me Learn

Bring to class things that help you learn.

10 Using Numbers

A. Listen. Use the number cards.

B. Practice numbers. **Look** at pages 125–128.

C. Listen. (Circle) the number.

1.	1	5	⑨
2.	3	5	12
3.	10	6	2
4.	11	7	4
5.	20	13	15
6.	13	30	3
7.	8	80	8
8.	50	15	5

D. Listen. Write the numbers.

1. _12_ **2.** _____ **3.** _____

4. _____ **5.** _____ **6.** _____

E. Write the numbers.

1. My classroom has _____ tape recorders.

2. My classroom has _____ pictures.

3. My classroom has _____ desks.

4. My classroom has _____ chairs.

5. My classroom has _____ maps.

F. Write.

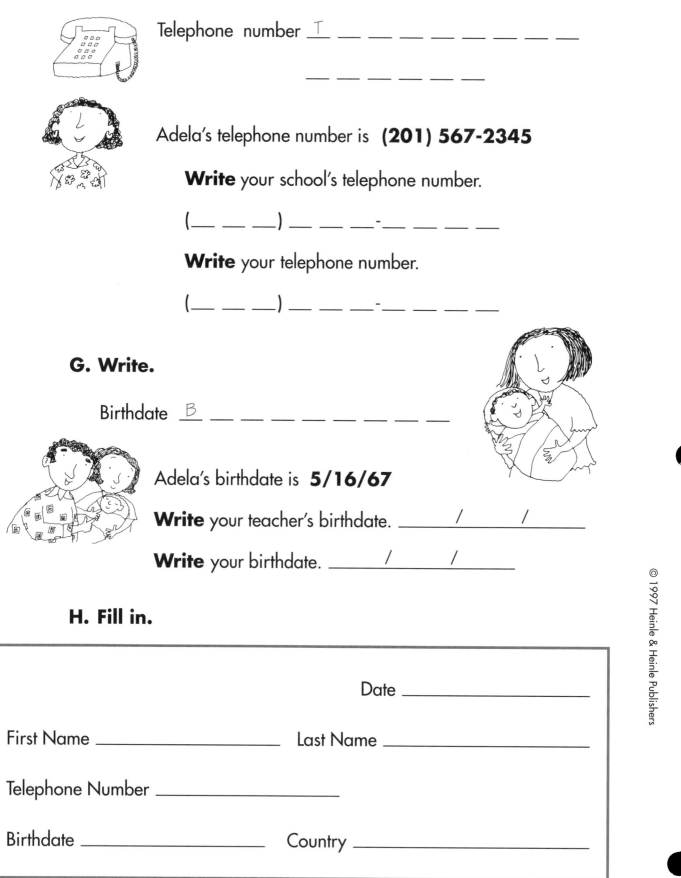

Telephone number T __ __ __ __ __ __ __ __ __

__ __ __ __ __ __

Adela's telephone number is **(201) 567-2345**

Write your school's telephone number.

(__ __ __) __ __ __-__ __ __ __

Write your telephone number.

(__ __ __) __ __ __-__ __ __ __

G. Write.

Birthdate B __ __ __ __ __ __ __ __ __

Adela's birthdate is **5/16/67**

Write your teacher's birthdate. _____ / _____ / _____

Write your birthdate. _____ / _____ / _____

H. Fill in.

Date _____

First Name _____ Last Name _____

Telephone Number _____

Birthdate _____ Country _____

© 1997 Heinle & Heinle Publishers

Picture Story: Edward

A. Look at the pictures. What do you see?

1.

2.

3.

4.

B. Listen to the story.

C. Tell the story to your partner.

© 1997 Heinle & Heinle Publishers

••• 35

Ideas for Action

A   B

A: May I have your phone number?

B: 303-5515.

A: Excuse me?

B: 303-5515.

A: Thank you.

A. Ask your classmates.

Name	Telephone Number

0 1 2 3 4 5 6 7 8 9

© 1997 Heinle & Heinle Publishers

Timeline

A. Look at the timeline.
Listen to Adela's story.

1967

1980
I finished grade 6.

1986

Now.
I can read some English.

1988

1995
I started English class.

B. Make more pictures of your life.
Put all your pictures in order.

C. Show the class your timeline.

Checklist for Learning

Check (✔) the words you know.

_____ blackboard	_____ listen	_____ always
_____ book	_____ speak	_____ often
_____ desk	_____ read	_____ sometimes
_____ map	_____ write	_____ never
_____ picture	_____ birthdate	_____ _____
_____ tape recorder	_____ telephone number	_____ _____

Check (✔) what you can do.

_____ read stories	_____ tell about my life
_____ write my story	_____ say numbers
_____ write numbers	_____ say my telephone number
_____ write my birthdate	_____ tell my birthdate
_____ write my telephone number	

Write the page numbers.

I liked pages _____.

I did not like pages _____.

© 1997 Heinle & Heinle Publishers

Unit

Narin's Story

Listen.

Narin Sao is from Cambodia.
He lives in Lowell, Massachusetts.

Play with the Story

A. Listen and **read.**

Every night I listen to songs from my country.
In my mind, I see my grandparents' farm.
There's no place like home.

B. Copy the story.

_____

_____

_____

_____

C. Say the words in the box. **Circle** the words in the story above.

country	listen	see	home	grandparents'

D. Write the missing words.

Every night I _____ to songs from my ___country___.

In my mind I _____ my _____ farm.

There's no place like _____.

3 Family: Near and Far Away

A. Look at Narin's family. Who lives <u>near</u>? Who lives <u>far away</u>?

PICTURE DICTIONARY

Narin's Family: in the U.S.A.

Narin's Family: in Cambodia

B. Copy the words.   **Write** the country.

Family		Country
wife	_wife_	U.S.A.
daughter	_____	_____
son	_____	_____
mother	_____	_____
father	_____	_____
sister	_____	_____
brother	_____	_____
grandparents	_____	_____

© 1997 Heinle & Heinle Publishers

C. Make your own picture dictionary.
Draw pictures of your family. **Label** the family members.

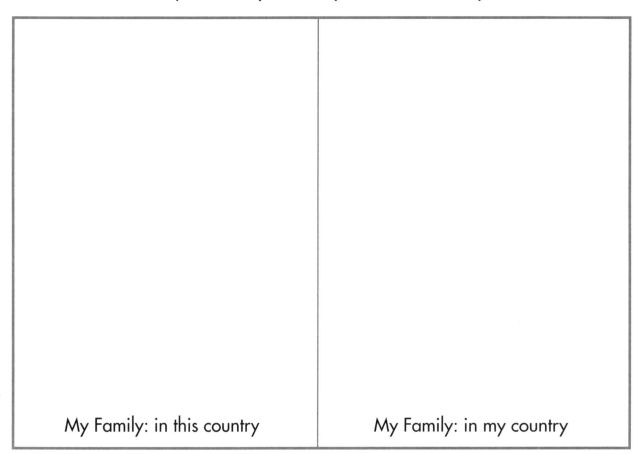

My Family: in this country	My Family: in my country

D. Write about your family. (Circle) Near or Far Away.

Family Members	Country	Near or Far Away
		Near Far Away
		Near Far Away
		Near Far Away
		Near Far Away
		Near Far Away

> Every night I listen to songs from my country.
> In my mind, I see my grandparents' farm.
> There's no place like home.

E. Read Narin's story again. **Circle** Yes or No.

1. Narin listens to songs from his country. (Yes)   No

2. Narin listens to songs in English. Yes   No

3. He thinks about his family far away. Yes   No

4. For Narin, Cambodia is home. Yes   No

5. For Narin, the U.S. is home. Yes   No

 F. Check your answers with the class.

G. Think about yourself. **Circle** Yes or No.

I listen to songs from my country.	Yes	No
I listen to songs in English.	Yes	No
I think about my family far away.	Yes	No
My country is home.	Yes	No
The U.S. is home.	Yes	No

H. Copy your *Yes* sentences.

_____

_____

_____

_____

 **I. Show** a partner.

Family Members

A. Look at the pictures.
What do you see?

B. Look at the words.
Label the pictures.

baby
mother
father
daughter
son
husband
wife
grandmother
grandchildren

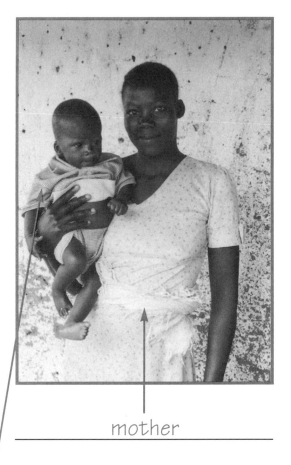

mother

_____

_____

_____

_____

_____

_____

© 1997 Heinle & Heinle Publishers

_____

_____

_____

_____

C. Label other things you see.

D. Show a partner.

E. Count. Write the numbers.

_2_ boys		_____ girls		_____ children	
_____ men		_____ women		_____ parents	
_____ males		_____ females		_____ grandparents	

5 My Teacher

A: Do you have brothers?

B: Yes.

A: How many?

B: I have 2 brothers.

A. Ask about your teacher's family.

Do You Have . . . ?	Circle One		How Many?
brothers	Yes	No	
sisters	Yes	No	
sons	Yes	No	
daughters	Yes	No	
	Yes	No	
	Yes	No	

B. Listen. Use the number cards.

C. Read and **say** the words.

Sex: Female
        She

Male
He

D. Listen. Use the letter cards.

46 •••

E. Write the missing letters.

Who is **she**?

Who is **he**?

m _o_ _t_ _h_ _e_ _r_

father

sister

b _ _ _ _ _ _

d _ _ _ _ _ _ _

son

wife

h _ _ _ _ _ _

g _ _ _ _ _ _ _ _ _

grandfather

woman

m _ _

g _ _ _

boy

F. Look at pictures of your teacher's family.
    Ask for the names.

A: Who is **she**?

B: **She** is my daughter.

A: What is **her** name?

B: Emily.

6 My Partner

A. Look at family photos or pictures with a partner.

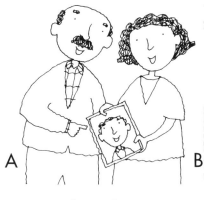

A   B

A: Who is **he**?
B: **He** is my brother.

A: What is **his** name?
B: Lee.

A: Spell that please.
B: L - E - E

A   B

A: Who is **she**?
B: **She** is my sister Mary.

A: Where does **she** live?
B: In Canada.

A: Spell that please.
B: C - A - N - A - D - A

B. Write about a partner's family.

Family Members	Name	Country
brothers		
sisters		
children		
parents		

Where You Live

A. **Copy** the words.

🏙	City	_City_
🗺	State	_State_
🌍	Country	_____
👶🌍	Birthplace	_____

B. **Look** at pictures of Adela.

Here is where Adela lives now.

Miami, Florida, U.S.A.

Here is Adela's birthplace.

La Union, El Salvador

C. **Write** where you live now.

I live in _____ .
City   State   Country

D. **Write** your birthplace.

I was born in _____ .
City   Country

E. **Write** your partner's birthplace.

My partner was born in _____ .
City   Country

8 Fatima's Story

A. Listen.

Fatima Gredelj lives in Atlanta, Georgia.

 B. Listen and **read.**

> I live in the U.S. I am from Bosnia.
> My husband, 2 sons and 8 grandchildren are not here.
> If all my family comes here, I can stay in the U.S.
> for 5 years, 10 years, or 20 years.
> I can live anywhere. But I want all my children with me.

C. (Circle) the words you know in the story.
   Write new words in the box.

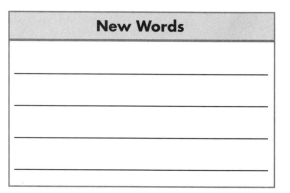

New Words

D. Read the story again. (Circle) the correct answer.

1. Does Fatima live in the <u>U.S.</u> or <u>Bosnia</u>?	(U.S.)	Bosnia
2. Is Fatima's birthplace the <u>U.S.</u> or <u>Bosnia</u>?	U.S.	Bosnia
3. Is Fatima's husband <u>here</u> or in <u>another country</u>?	here	another country
4. Does Fatima have <u>daughters</u> or <u>sons</u> in Bosnia?	daughters	sons
5. Does she have a <u>grandchild</u> or <u>grandchildren</u>?	grandchild	grandchildren

E. Check your answers with the class.

F. Think about yourself. (Circle) Yes or No.

I live in the U.S.	Yes	No
I want to stay here in the U.S.	Yes	No
I don't want to stay here.	Yes	No
Part of my family is here.	Yes	No
Part of my family is not here.	Yes	No
I want my children with me.	Yes	No
I want my parents with me.	Yes	No

G. Copy your *Yes* sentences.

_____

_____

_____

_____

 **H. Show** a partner.

A. Look at the pictures. What do you see?

1.
Laos

2.
Laos

3.
Laos

4.
My Country
U.S.

5.
Come to America!
U.S.

6.
U.S.

B. Listen to the story.

C. Tell the story to a partner.

 My Address

A. Copy the words.

Address	_____ Address _____
Street	_____ Street _____ St. _____
Apartment	_____ Apt. _Apt._
ZIP Code	_____ ZIP _____

B. Fill in the form.

Name: _____

Address: _____

            Number   Street   Apt.

          _____

            City   State   ZIP

Telephone: _____

Birthplace: _____   Sex: Male   Female

Married?   Yes   No   Children?   Yes   No

C. Practice using envelopes. Look at page 129.

:11: Ideas for Action

A. Think about your family far away.
Adela writes a letter to her mother.

Here is the address: _Rosa Lopez_
Calle 24, Apartado 36
La Union, El Salvador   C.A.

B. Write names of family members you want to contact.

1. Who can you write a letter to?

I can write a letter to _____.

Here is the address: _____

_____

_____

Come
to
America!

2. Who can you call on the telephone?

I can call _____ on the telephone.

Here is the telephone number: _____

3. Who can you visit?

I can visit _____.

Here is the name of the city: _____

54 • • •

© 1997 Heinle & Heinle Publishers

Timeline

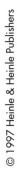

A. Look at the timeline.
Listen to Adela's story.

1967

1980

1986

1995 — Run Eat Ran Ate

19

Now

1990 — *My daughter Eva was born.*

1993 — David Lopez 1923–1993 — *My father died.*

Don't do

B. Make more pictures of your life.
Put all your pictures in order.

C. Show the class your timeline.

Checklist for Learning

Check (✔) the words you know.

_____ mother	_____ woman	_____ address	_____
_____ father	_____ man	_____ street	_____
_____ sister	_____ girl	_____ apartment	_____
_____ brother	_____ boy	_____ city	_____
_____ daughter	_____ child	_____ state	_____
_____ son	_____ children	_____ ZIP code	_____
_____ wife	_____ sex	_____ birthplace	_____
_____ husband	_____ female	_____ call	
_____ baby	_____ male	_____ write	
_____ grandparents		_____ visit	
_____ grandchildren			

Check (✔) what you can do.

_____ read stories	_____ tell about my life
_____ write my story	_____ tell about my family
_____ write my address	_____ tell where my family lives
_____ write about birthplace	_____ tell my birthplace
_____ write family words	_____ _____

Write the page numbers.

I liked pages _____ .

I did not like pages _____ .

Unit 4

1 Ramon's Story

Listen.

Ramon Ramirez is from Mexico.
He works in Santa Fe, New Mexico.

Play with the Story

A. Listen and **read.**

I start work at 5:00 in the morning.
I work from 5:00 A.M. to 1:30 P.M.
Sometimes I work from 5:00 A.M. to 5:00 P.M.!

B. Copy the story.

_____

_____

_____

_____

C. Say the words in the box. **Circle** the words in the story above.

morning	to	work	from	start

D. Write the missing words.

I _____ work at 5:00 in the ____morning____.

I work _____ 5:00 A.M. to 1:30 P.M.

Sometimes I _____ from 5:00 A.M. _____ 5:00 P.M.!

A.M.		P.M.	
From midnight	To noon	From noon	To midnight

E. **Look** at Ramon's work day.
Listen to the time.   **Write** the time. (**Circle**) A.M. or P.M.

Ramon always starts work at _____ : _____   A.M.   P.M.

Ramon often finishes work at _____ : _____   A.M.   P.M.

Ramon sometimes finishes work at _____ : _____   A.M.   P.M.

F. **Listen** and **use** the clock.

G. Practice using clocks. **Look** at pages 134–136.

3 ... ight

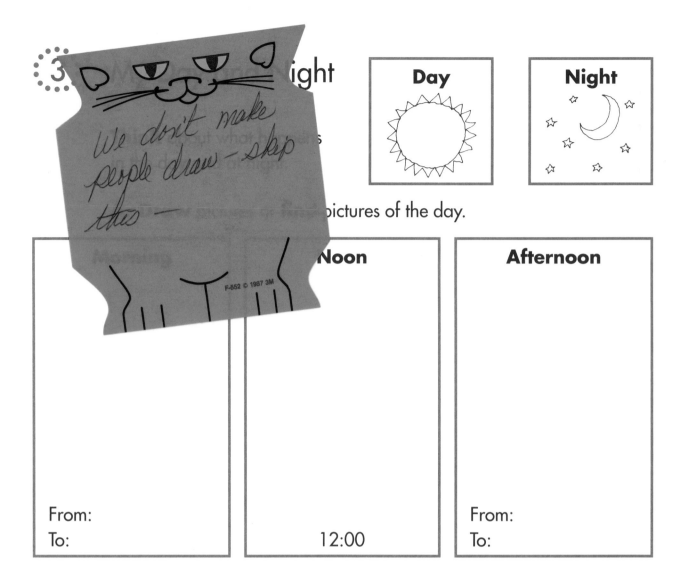

Day

Night

... pictures of the day.

Morning	Noon	Afternoon
From: To:	12:00	From: To:

Handwritten note: We don't make ... people draw – skip this —

F-552 © 1987 3M

B. Draw pictures or **find** pictures of the night.

Evening	Night	Midnight
From: To:	From: To:	12:00

60 ...

I start work at 5:00 in the morning.
I work from 5:00 A.M. to 1:30 P.M.
Sometimes I work from 5:00 A.M. to 5:00 P.M.!

C. Read Ramon's story again.
(Circle) Yes or No.

1. Ramon always starts work at 5:00 in the morning.	(Yes)	No
2. Ramon starts work at 5:00 P.M.	Yes	No
3. He finishes in the afternoon.	Yes	No
4. He always finishes work at 1:30 P.M.	Yes	No
5. He sometimes finishes work at 5:00 P.M.	Yes	No

 D. Check your answers with the class.

E. Think about yourself. (Circle) Yes or No.

I have a job.	Yes	No
I do housework at home.	Yes	No
I start work in the morning.	Yes	No
I start work in the afternoon.	Yes	No
I start work in the evening.	Yes	No
I finish work in the morning.	Yes	No
I finish work in the afternoon.	Yes	No
I finish work in the evening.	Yes	No

F. Copy your *Yes* sentences.

_____

_____

_____

_____

G. Show a partner.

H. Think about yourself.   **Write** the time.   (Circle) A.M. or P.M.
Copy the sentence.

I **get up** at ____ : ____ .   A.M.   P.M.

_____

I **leave home** at ____ : ____ .   A.M.   P.M.

_____

I **start school** at ____ : ____ .   A.M.   P.M.

_____

I **finish school** at ____ : ____ .   A.M.   P.M.

_____

I **get home** at ____ : ____ .   A.M.   P.M.

_____

I **go to bed** at ____ : ____ .   A.M.   P.M.

_____

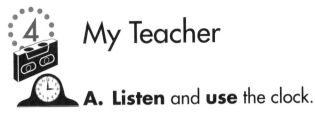

My Teacher

A. Listen and **use** the clock.

B. Listen to your teacher.   **Write** the time.   **Draw** the hands.
Copy the sentence.   **Circle** A.M. or P.M.

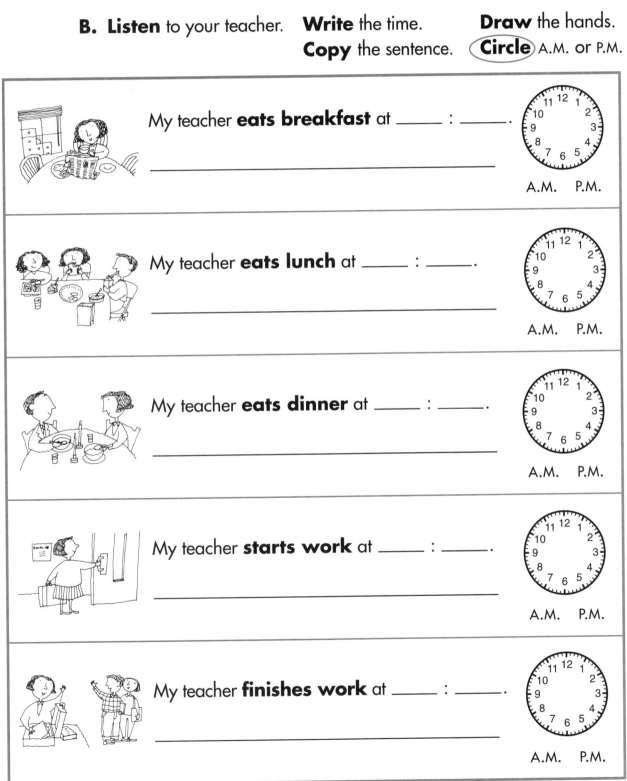

My teacher **eats breakfast** at _____ : _____.

_____

A.M.   P.M.

My teacher **eats lunch** at _____ : _____.

_____

A.M.   P.M.

My teacher **eats dinner** at _____ : _____.

_____

A.M.   P.M.

My teacher **starts work** at _____ : _____.

_____

A.M.   P.M.

My teacher **finishes work** at _____ : _____.

_____

A.M.   P.M.

5 Jobs

A. Look at the pictures.
What do you see?

B. Look at the words.
Label the pictures.

construction worker
custodian
driver
mechanic
seamstress
secretary

64 •••

C. Label other things you see.

D. Show a partner.

E. Which jobs are **day** jobs?
Which jobs are **night** jobs?

 **My Partner**

A. Read the days of the week. **Copy** the words.

Sunday	_____	Sun.	_____
Monday	_____	Mon.	_____
Tuesday	_____	Tues.	_____
Wednesday	_____	Wed.	_____
Thursday	_____	Thurs.	_____
Friday	_____	Fri.	_____
Saturday	_____	Sat.	_____

B. Ask about a partner's days.   **Write** the time.

A: What time do you get up on Sunday?
B: I get up at 9:30 A.M.

A: What time do you go to bed on Sunday?
B: I go to bed at 10:30 P.M.

	Get Up	Go to Bed
Sun.	___ : ___	___ : ___
Mon.	___ : ___	___ : ___
Tues.	___ : ___	___ : ___
Wed.	___ : ___	___ : ___
Thurs.	___ : ___	___ : ___
Fri.	___ : ___	___ : ___
Sat.	___ : ___	___ : ___

© 1997 Heinle & Heinle Publishers

 C. Listen and use the calendar cards.

Work You Do

A. **Copy** the words.

PICTURE DICTIONARY

build   _____build_____

cook   _____

clean   _____

drive   _____

fix a car   _____ _____ _____

make calls   _____ _____

sew   _____

watch children   _____ _____

B. Make your own Picture Dictionary.
Find pictures or **draw** pictures of work you do.

C. Write the work you do.

My Housework	My Job
_____	_____
_____	_____
_____	_____

A. Listen.

Chung Spears is from Korea.
She lives in Charleston, West Virginia.

 B. Listen and **read.**

I leave my school at 1:30 in the afternoon.
I pick up my boys at 2:30 P.M.
Then, I clean my house.
I watch my boys play.
In the evening I cook dinner.
My boys eat. They take a shower.
They go to bed at 8:00 o'clock.

C. (Circle) the words you know in the story.
   Write new words in the box.

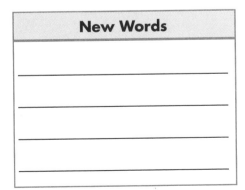

New Words

D. Read the story again. (Circle) the correct answer.

1. Does she leave school in the <u>morning</u> or <u>afternoon</u>?   morning   (afternoon)

2. Does Chung leave school at <u>1:30 A.M.</u> or <u>1:30 P.M.</u>?   A.M.   P.M.

3. Does she <u>go home</u> or <u>go to a job</u>?   home   job

4. Does Chung <u>do housework</u> or <u>have a job</u>?   housework   job

5. Does she cook <u>breakfast</u> or <u>dinner</u> in the evening?   breakfast   dinner

✓ **E. Check** your answers with the class.

F. Think about yourself. (Circle) Yes or No

I clean the house.	Yes	No
I don't clean the house.	Yes	No
I cook for my family.	Yes	No
I cook for myself.	Yes	No
I don't cook.	Yes	No
I do housework.	Yes	No
I never do housework.	Yes	No
I never finish my housework.	Yes	No

G. Copy your *Yes* sentences.

_____

_____

_____

_____

 **H. Show** a partner.

70 ...

© 1997 Heinle & Heinle Publishers

9 Picture Story: Lora

A. Look at the pictures. What do you see?

1. 7:00 P.M.

2. 8:00 P.M.

3. 4:30 A.M.

4. 5:15 A.M.

5. 6:30 A.M.

6. 8:30 A.M.

B. Listen to the story.

C. Tell the story to your partner.

© 1997 Heinle & Heinle Publishers

... 71

Work Schedules

A. Write your <u>work</u> or <u>school</u> schedule.   **Draw** the clock hands.

	start	finish	start	finish
S	___ : ___	___ : ___		
M	___ : ___	___ : ___		
T	___ : ___	___ : ___		
W	___ : ___	___ : ___		
T	___ : ___	___ : ___		
F	___ : ___	___ : ___		
S	___ : ___	___ : ___		

 **B. Show** a partner.

© 1997 Heinle & Heinle Publishers

 **Job Forms**

A. **Copy** the words.

Work	_W o r k_	_____
Job	_ _ _	_____ _Job_ _____
Hours	_ _ _ _ _	_____
Schedule	_ _ _ _ _ _ _ _	_____

B. **Fill in** the form.

Personal Information:

Name: _____

Address: _____
            Number   Street   Apt.

            _____
            City   State   ZIP

Telephone: _____ _____
            Home Phone   Work Phone

Work:

Do you have a job?   Yes   No

Work you do: _____

Schedule:

Circle all work days: Mon.   Tues.   Wed.   Thurs.   Fri.   Sat.   Sun.

Work hours: From _____   To _____

C. **Tell** a partner.

A. Look at the pictures. ~~**Cross out**~~ what makes you <u>tired</u>.

B. Look at the pictures. (**Circle**) what helps you <u>relax</u>.

building	fishing	taking a bath
cleaning	fixing a car	taking a nap
cooking	listening to music	taking a shower
dancing	sewing	watching children
driving	shopping	watching TV

C. Write what helps you <u>relax</u>.

_____   _____

_____   _____

 **D. Show a** partner.

Timeline

A. Look at the timeline.
Listen to Adela's story.

1967

1980

1982
I worked in a restaurant.

1986

1987

1988

1990

1991
I was a babysitter.

1992
I worked in a hotel.

1993
David Lopez 1923–1993

1995
Run Eat Ran Ate

Now

B. Make more pictures of your life.
Put all your pictures in order.

C. Show the class your timeline.

Checklist for Learning

Check (✔) the words you know.

_____ start	_____ morning	_____ Monday
_____ finish	_____ noon	_____ Tuesday
_____ get up	_____ afternoon	_____ Wednesday
_____ go to bed	_____ evening	_____ Thursday
_____ leave	_____ night	_____ Friday
_____ get home	_____ midnight	_____ Saturday
_____ breakfast	_____ A.M.	_____ Sunday
_____ lunch	_____ P.M.	_____ _____
_____ dinner	_____ clock	_____ _____
_____ job	_____ schedule	_____ _____
_____ work	_____ _____	_____ _____

Check (✔) what you can do.

_____ read stories	_____ tell about my life
_____ write my story	_____ say the days of the week
_____ write about my day	_____ tell about my day
_____ write the time	_____ say the time
_____ write the days of the week	_____ _____

Write the page numbers.

I liked pages _____ .

I did not like pages _____ .

Unit 5

 1 Avelino Gonzalez's Story

Listen.

Avelino Gonzalez is from Cuba.
He lives in Miami, Florida.

© 1997 Heinle & Heinle Publishers

Play with the Story

A. Listen and read.

In Little Havana in Miami, I can find everything from my country—
Cuban coffee, mangoes, papayas, and pineapples.
I can find my people, too.
It feels like home!

B. Copy the story.

_____

_____

_____

_____

_____

C. Say the words in the box. (Circle) the words in the story above.

country	coffee	and	people	home

D. Write the missing words.

In little Havana in Miami, I can find everything from my ___country___ —

Cuban _____, mangoes, papayas, _____ pineapples. I

can find my _____ too.

It feels like _____!

E. (Circle) Yes or No.

1. Avelino lives in Miami.   (Yes)   No

2. Avelino is from Cuba.   Yes   No

3. Avelino can find everything from his country.   Yes   No

4. He can find his people.   Yes   No

5. He can find mangoes.   Yes   No

6. He can find pineapples.   Yes   No

7. Little Havana in Miami feels like school.   Yes   No

 F. Check your answers with the class.

G. Think about yourself.

What is the name of your city? _____

Can you find your people in your city? _____

Does your city feel like home? _____

H. Tell your answers to a partner.

Foods

A. Copy the words.

PICTURE DICTIONARY

apples ___apples___

cake _____

carrots _____

chicken _____

coffee _____

eggs _____

fish _____

pears _____

B. Make your own picture dictionary.
   Find pictures or **draw** pictures of foods you eat.

C. Write the foods you like and don't like.

I Like	I Don't Like
_____	_____
_____	_____
_____	_____

(4) My Teacher

A. Listen to your teacher.
Circle the foods she likes. ~~Cross out~~ the foods she doesn't like.

 B. Listen. Use the alphabet cards.

5 Shopping: Money Practice

We have money to count

A. Listen. Use the money cards.

B. Practice counting money. **Look** at pages 130–132.

C. Count, write, and **say.**

50¢

_____   _____   _____

_____   _____   _____

D. Listen. Circle the prices you hear.

1. $5.00	5¢	($15.00)
2. $1.50	50¢	5¢
3. $10.10	$1.00	1¢
4. $15.08	80¢	$15.18
5. 65¢	56¢	$5.00

E. Listen and **write** the prices.

1. ___$2.44___   **2.** _____   **3.** _____

4. _____   **5.** _____   **6.** _____

F. Check your answers with the class.

G. In class choose a food to find at the supermarket.

Food _____

Go to your supermarket.
How much does it cost?

_____

Tell the class the price.

STOP AND SHOP
Pears
59¢ lb

A&C SUPERMARKET
Pears
65¢ lb

MARIO'S MARKET
Pears
69¢ lb

Classmate	Store	Price

© 1997 Heinle & Heinle Publishers

Are the prices the <u>same</u> or <u>different</u>?

H. Look at Adela's money order.
She writes a money order to her school.

First Bank Money Order   Date ___*April 18*___ 19 _96_

••••••••••••••••••••**$100.00**••••••••••••••••••••

One hundred and 00/100 dollars

Pay to the order of ___County Adult School___

From: ___Adela Flores___
Name
___125 West Street___
Street
___Miami, Florida 33520___
City   State   Zip code

She writes the school name here.   She writes her name and address here.

How much is the money order for? _____

I. Fill in the money order. Pay it to your school.

First Bank Money Order   Date ___*April 18*___ 19 _96_

••••••••••••••••••••**$50.00**••••••••••••••••••••

Fifty and 00/100 dollars

Pay to the order of _____

From: _____
Name

_____
Street

_____
City   State   Zip code

A. Look at the pictures. What do you see?

B. Look at the words. **Label** the pictures.

bank
post office
supermarket
laundromat
hospital
park

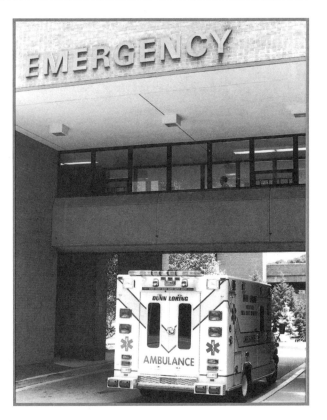

C. Label other things you see.

D. Show a partner.

7 My Neighborhood

A. Listen. (Circle) places you hear.

1.

2.

3.

4.

 B. Check your answers with the class.

C. Check ✔ the places you have in your neighborhood.

_____ hospital   _____ post office   _____ supermarket

_____ bank   _____ laundromat   _____ park

 **D. Tell** a partner.

Picture Story: Mrs. Kim

A. Look at the pictures. What do you see?

1.

2.

3.

MOVERS

4.

5.

MOVERS

6.

7.

8.

B. Listen to the story.

C. Tell the story to a partner.

Where do people meet and talk in your neighborhood?

A. Draw a picture of places people meet in your neighborhood.

B. Show the class.

10 The Farmer's Market

A. Listen.

B. Listen and **read.**

I sell food at the Farmer's Market.
The Farmer's Market is outdoors.
It is open every Saturday from 7:00 A.M. to 12:00 P.M.
People buy fresh fruits and vegetables.
I sell a lot of lettuce, tomatoes, and corn.

Karin Boyd is from the United States.

New Words
_____
_____
_____
_____
_____

C. (Circle) the words you know in the story.
Write new words in the box.

D. Read the story again. (Circle) the correct answer.

1. Is the Farmer's Market open on <u>Saturday</u>
or <u>Sunday</u>?   (Saturday)   Sunday

2. Is the Farmer's Market <u>outdoors</u> or <u>indoors</u>?   outdoors   indoors

3. Do they sell <u>coffee</u> or <u>lettuce</u>?   coffee   lettuce

4. Does it open at <u>6:00</u> or <u>7:00</u>?   6:00   7:00

 **E. Check** your answers with the class.

F. Think about yourself.
(Circle) Yes or No.

I go shopping at a farmer's market.	Yes	No
I go shopping in the supermarket.	Yes	No
I buy fresh vegetables.	Yes	No
I buy fresh fruits.	Yes	No
I buy tomatoes.	Yes	No
I buy papayas.	Yes	No
I have outdoor markets in my country.	Yes	No

G. Copy your *Yes* sentences.

_____

_____

_____

_____

_____

_____

 **H. Show** a partner.

Timeline

A. Look at the timeline. **Listen** to Adela's story.

1967

1980

1982

1986

1987

1988

1990

1991

1992

1993

1994 — *I moved to Miami, Florida.*

1995

Now.

David Lopez 1923–1993

Welcome to Miami

Run Eat Ran Ate

B. Make more pictures of your life.
Put all your pictures in order.

C. Show the class your timeline.

Checklist for Learning

Check (✔) the words you know.

_____ apples	_____ penny	_____ bank
_____ cake	_____ nickel	_____ hospital
_____ carrots	_____ dime	_____ laundromat
_____ chicken	_____ quarter	_____ park
_____ coffee	_____ dollar	_____ post office
_____ eggs	_____ _____	_____ supermarket
_____ fish	_____ _____	_____ _____
_____ pears	_____ _____	_____ _____

Check (✔) what you can do.

_____ read stories	_____ say prices
_____ write about myself	_____ tell about my life
_____ write a money order	_____ tell about my neighborhood
_____ write prices	_____ tell about foods I like and do not like

Write the page numbers.

I liked pages _____.

I did not like pages _____.

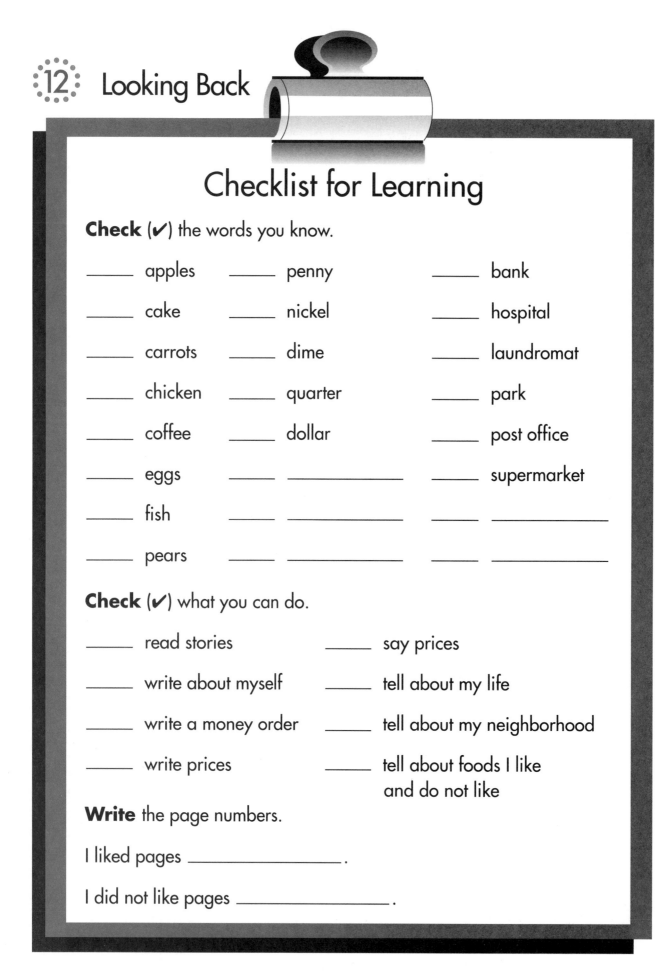

Unit 6

Susanna's Story

Listen.

Lesli

brush

Lesli studied in Susanna's class at the ABC School in Cerritos, California.

2 Play with the Story

A. **Listen** and **read**.

Our school had a celebration at the end of the year.
Students decorated a room.
They taught about their countries.
Lesli taught about the Chinese language.

Susanna Levitt, Teacher
ABC School

B. **Copy** the story.

_____

_____

_____

_____

_____

C. **Say** the words in the box. **Circle** the words in the story above.

celebration	countries	school	taught	Students

D. **Write** the missing words.

Our _____*school*_____ had a _____ at

the end of the year.

_____ decorated a room.

They taught about their _____.

Lesli _____ about the Chinese language.

© 1997 Heinle & Heinle Publishers

E. (Circle) Yes or No.

1. Susanna's school had a celebration every day.   Yes   (No)

2. Susanna's school had a celebration at the end.   Yes   No

3. Students decorated a room.   Yes   No

4. Students decorated their homes.   Yes   No

5. They taught about their families.   Yes   No

6. They taught about their countries.   Yes   No

7. Lesli taught about the English language.   Yes   No

8. Lesli taught about the Chinese language.   Yes   No

F. Check your answers with the class.

G. Think about yourself.

At my school we celebrate ————————————————————.

I can teach about ————————————————————.

My Celebration

A. Think about a celebration or holiday.
   Check (✔) what you did.

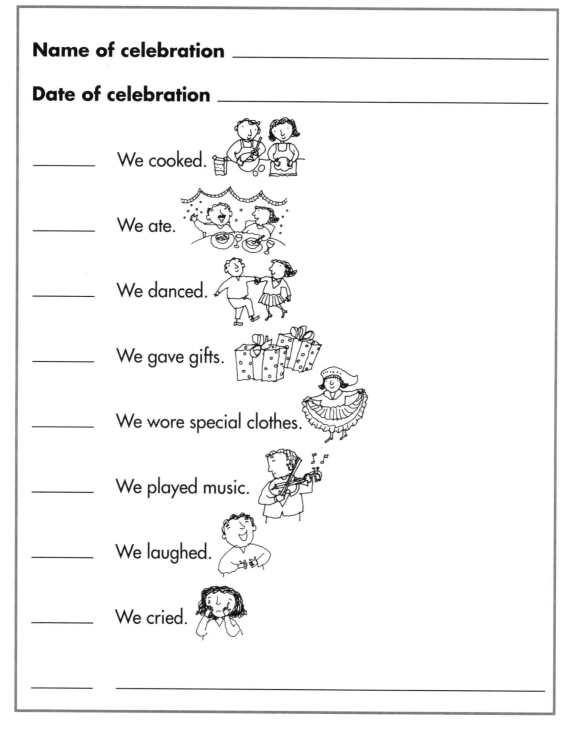

Name of celebration _____

Date of celebration _____

_____ We cooked.

_____ We ate.

_____ We danced.

_____ We gave gifts.

_____ We wore special clothes.

_____ We played music.

_____ We laughed.

_____ We cried.

_____ _____

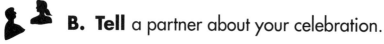 **B. Tell** a partner about your celebration.

C. **Match** the words and pictures.

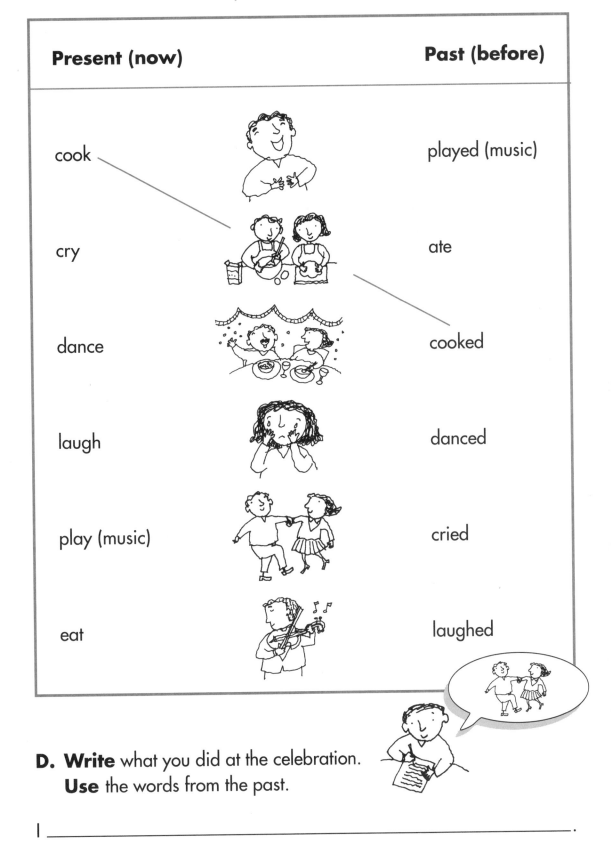

Present (now)	Past (before)
cook	played (music)
cry	ate
dance	cooked
laugh	danced
play (music)	cried
eat	laughed

D. **Write** what you did at the celebration. **Use** the words from the past.

I _____.

I _____.

4 My Teacher

A. Listen. **Use** the number cards.

B. Practice using dates on page 138.

C. Listen to your teacher.
  Check (✔) what your teacher did.

Name of celebration _____

Date of celebration _____

_____ cooked   _____ wore special clothes

_____ danced   _____ laughed

_____ ate   _____ cried

_____ played music   _____ _____

D. What did you learn about your teacher?
  Tell a partner.

A: What did the teacher do?

B: She cooked fish.

© 1997 Heinle & Heinle Publishers

Our Celebrations

A: What's this?

B: It's a piñata.

A. Bring a picture or photo of your celebration.
Bring something you wear, eat, or use.

B. Tell the class about your celebration.

C. Draw a picture of what you do for your celebration.

A. Plan your celebration with the class.

(Circle) Yes or No.

Tell your ideas to the class.

Who are we going to invite?		
Our families	Yes	No
Our neighbors	Yes	No

What are we going to eat?		
Food from our countries	Yes	No
Drinks	Yes	No

What are we going to do?		
sing and dance	Yes	No
teach songs, dances	Yes	No
listen to music	Yes	No

What are we going to bring?		
tape recorder	Yes	No
guitar	Yes	No
other instruments	Yes	No

B. Work with a group of students.
Think about what you will do.
Write the names and information.

Will you bring something?

Will you teach something?

Will you cook something?

Name	What will you bring, teach, or cook?

C. Tell the class what your group wrote.

D. Write what you will do. _____

E. After the party:
Write a class story.

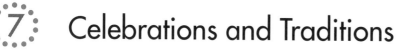

Celebrations and Traditions

A. Look at the pictures.
What do you see?

B. Look at the words.
Label the pictures.

playing music
traditional dancing
going in the temple
marching in a parade
welcoming visitors

C. Label other things you see.

 **D. Show** a partner.

Holidays

A. Copy the words.

PICTURE DICTIONARY

New Year's Day _____ New Year's Day _____

Valentine's Day _____

Mother's Day _____

Independence Day _____

Thanksgiving _____

Christmas _____

© 1997 Heinle & Heinle Publishers

B. Make your own picture dictionary.
   Find pictures or draw pictures of holidays you like.

C. Label the holidays in your own picture dictionary.

© 1997 Heinle & Heinle Publishers

9 The Calendar

A. Listen. Use the alphabet cards.

B. Practice using the calendars on pages 136–138.

C. Work with the class.
Write the holidays on the calendar.

January	February	March	April
1–New Year's Day			
May	June	July	August
September	October	November	December

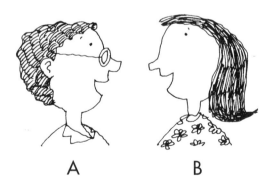

A   B

A: What's your favorite holiday?

B: My favorite holiday is New Year's Day.

A: What do you do?

B: We have a parade.

D. Tell your partner about your holidays.

E. Make a big calendar with your class.
Put a star ★ on the holidays.

© 1997 Heinle & Heinle Publishers

Seasons

A. Look at the pictures. **Say** the words.

B. Copy the words.

spring _ _ _ _ _ _ _____

_____

summer _ _ _ _ _ _ _____

_____

fall _ _ _ _ _____

_____

winter _ _ _ _ _ _ _____

_____

C. What is your favorite season?
    (Circle) what you can do in that season.

fish	play soccer	ski
swim	go to the beach	walk

I can fish.

:11: Monica's Story

  A. Listen.

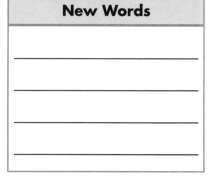

My name is Monica Salazar.
I am from Venezuela.
In class we talked about holidays.
One holiday I miss is Carnaval.
We take two days off work.
We can go to the beach.
We can stay home and rest.

Monica Salazar lives in
Charleston, West Virginia.

New Words

B. Listen and **read.**

C. (Circle) the words you know in the story.
Write new words in the box.

D. Read the story again. (Circle) the correct answer.

1. Is the story about <u>Monique</u> or <u>Monica</u>?   Monique   (Monica)

2. Is Monica from <u>Venezuela</u> or <u>Virginia</u>?   Venezuela   Virginia

3. Does Monica miss <u>Carnaval</u> or <u>Christmas</u>?   Carnaval   Christmas

4. Do people take off <u>two days</u> or <u>two weeks</u>?   two days   two weeks

 **E. Check** your answers with the class.

F. Think about yourself.
Circle Yes or No.

I am from Venezuela.	Yes	No
In class we talked about holidays.	Yes	No
I miss Carnaval.	Yes	No
I miss New Year's Day.	Yes	No
I like to go to the beach.	Yes	No
On holidays I can stay home and rest.	Yes	No
I liked talking about celebrations.	Yes	No

G. Copy your *Yes* sentences.

_____

_____

_____

_____

_____

_____

H. What do you miss from your country?
Circle the words.

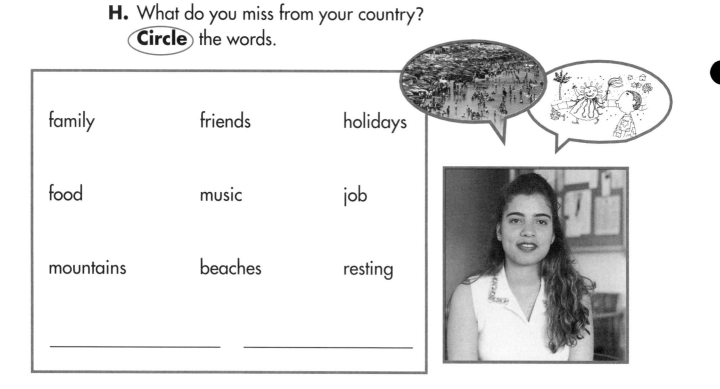

family	friends	holidays
food	music	job
mountains	beaches	resting

_____ _____

I. What do you like about this country?
Circle the words.

family	friends	holidays
food	music	job
mountains	beaches	resting

_____ _____

 **J. Tell** a partner what you think.

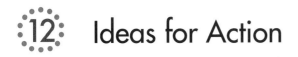

My grandmother spoke German when she was a girl.
She forgot how to speak it.
My mother never learned German.
I remember some special Christmas songs and stories.
I taught them to my children.
I hope they keep the songs and stories.

Lynda Terrill lives in Virginia.

Lynda's mother, Audrey Schmedlen, with her son, Roger, in 1943.

A. Think about traditions.
What traditions will you keep?
What traditions will you change?

B. Write two lists.

Keep	Change

C. Talk about your ideas with the class.

13 Picture Story: The Class

A. Look at the pictures. What do you see?

1.

2.   GATE A 7

3.

4.   TO GATE →

5.

6.   School Registration Tonight

7.

8.

B. Listen to the story.

C. Tell the story to your partner.

Timeline

A. Look at the timeline.
Listen to Adela's story.

1967

1980

1982

1986

1987

1988

1990

1991

1992

1993

1994

1995

1993
David Lopez
1923–1993

Future.

*My children will visit
El Salvador.*

Now.

B. Make more pictures of your life.
Put all your pictures in order.

C. Show the class your timeline.

Checklist for Learning

Check (✔) the words you know.

_____ cooked	_____ New Year's Day	_____ calendar
_____ ate	_____ Valentine's Day	_____ seasons
_____ danced	_____ Mother's Day	_____ spring
_____ gave	_____ Independence Day	_____ summer
_____ wore	_____ Thanksgiving Day	_____ fall
_____ played	_____ Christmas	_____ winter
_____ taught	_____ celebrations	_____ miss
_____ _____	_____ _____	_____ _____

Check (✔) what you can do.

_____ read stories	_____ tell about my life
_____ write my story	_____ tell about my celebrations
_____ write about celebrations	_____ tell about my holidays
_____ write holidays	_____ tell about what I miss
_____ use a calendar	_____ _____

Write the page numbers.

I liked pages _____.

I did not like pages _____.

© 1997 Heinle & Heinle Publishers

INDEX . . .

Aa	Bb	Cc	Dd	Ee	Ff	Gg	Hh	Ii	Jj
Kk	Ll	Mm	Nn	Oo	Pp	Qq	Rr	Ss	Tt
Uu	Vv	Ww	Xx	Yy	Zz				

A. Copy the capital letters.

A B C D E F G H I J K L M

A _ _ _ _ _ _ _ _ _ _ _ _

N O P Q R S T U V W X Y Z

_ _ _ _ _ _ _ _ _ _ _ _ _

B. Circle the letters of your first name.
Say the letters.

C. Copy the small letters.

a b c d e f g h i j k l m

a _ _ _ _ _ _ _ _ _ _ _ _

n o p q r s t u v w x y z

_ _ _ _ _ _ _ _ _ _ _ _ _

D. Circle the letters of your first name.
Say the letters.

Alphabet Practice 2

A. Copy the letters.

a a a ___ ___ ___ ___   n n ___ ___ ___ ___

b b ___ ___ ___ ___   o o ___ ___ ___ ___

c c ___ ___ ___ ___   p p ___ ___ ___ ___

d d ___ ___ ___ ___   q q ___ ___ ___ ___

e e ___ ___ ___ ___   r r ___ ___ ___ ___

f f ___ ___ ___ ___   s s ___ ___ ___ ___

g g ___ ___ ___ ___   t t ___ ___ ___ ___

h h ___ ___ ___ ___   u u ___ ___ ___ ___

i i ___ ___ ___ ___   v v ___ ___ ___ ___

j j ___ ___ ___ ___   w w ___ ___ ___ ___

k k ___ ___ ___ ___   x x ___ ___ ___ ___

l l ___ ___ ___ ___   y y ___ ___ ___ ___

m m ___ ___ ___ ___   z z ___ ___ ___ ___

Alphabet Practice 3

A. Match the capital and small letters.

1.		
A		i
B		d
C		g
D		a
E		h
F		b
G		f
H		c
I		e

2.		
J		n
K		l
L		p
M		m
N		j
O		q
P		r
Q		k
R		o

3.		
S		w
T		u
U		z
V		y
W		s
X		x
Y		t
Z		v

.... Alphabet Practice 4

A. Write the missing capital letters.

A   B   *C*   D   E   F   __   H   I   J   K   L   __

N   O   P   __   R   S   T   __   V   W   __   Y   Z

B. Write the missing small letters.

a   b   c   *d*   e   f   g   h   __   j   __   l   m

n   __   p   q   r   s   __   u   v   __   x   __   z

 **C. Practice** with the alphabet cards.
Put the alphabet cards in order.

D. Write your first and last name.
Spell it for your partner or your teacher.

_____   _____
first   last

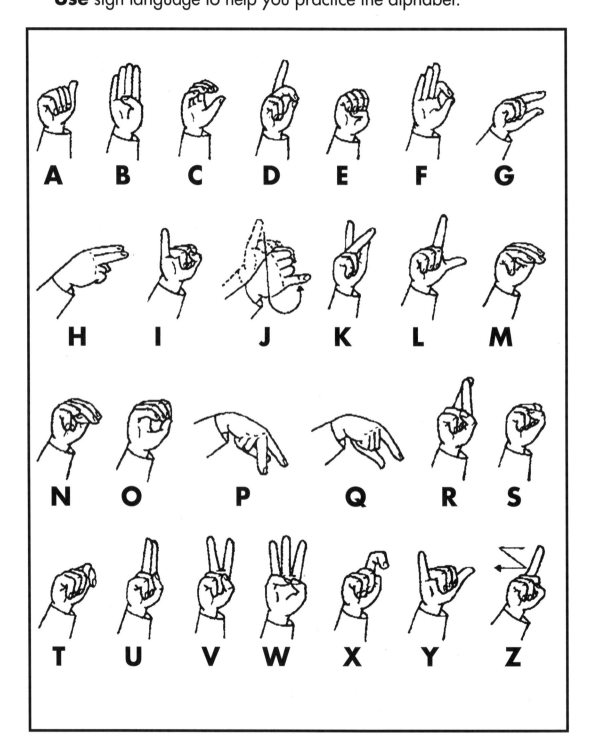

Alphabet Practice 5

A. Practice sign language with the class.
   Use sign language to help you practice the alphabet.

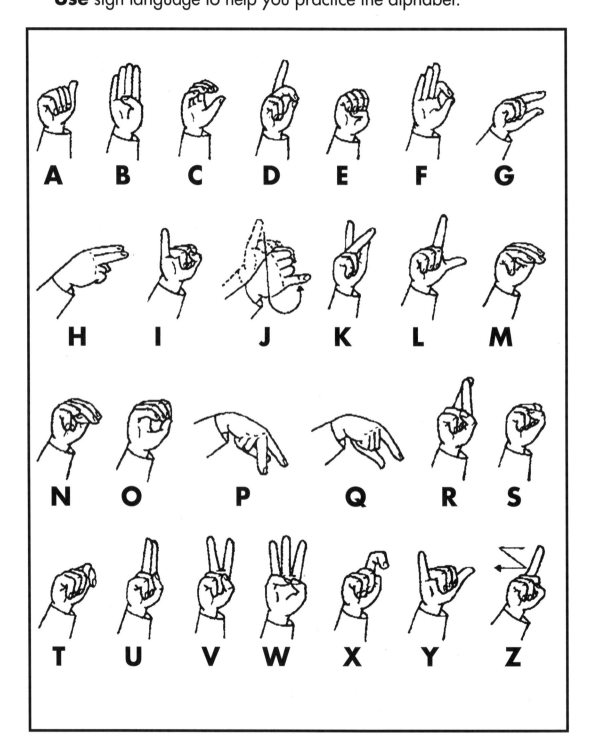

Say the numbers. **Write** the numbers.

0	0
1	1
2	2
3	3
4	4
5	5
6	6
7	7
8	8
9	9
10	10
11	11
12	12
13	13
14	14
15	15
16	16
17	17
18	18
19	19
20	20

······· Number Practice

A. Say the numbers.

1	2	3	4	5	6	7	8	9	10
11	12	13	14	15	16	17	18	19	20
21	22	23	24	25	26	27	28	29	30
31	32	33	34	35	36	37	38	39	40
41	42	43	44	45	46	47	48	49	50
51	52	53	54	55	56	57	58	59	60
61	62	63	64	65	66	67	68	69	70
71	72	73	74	75	76	77	78	79	80
81	82	83	84	85	86	87	88	89	90
91	92	93	94	95	96	97	98	99	100

B. Write the numbers.

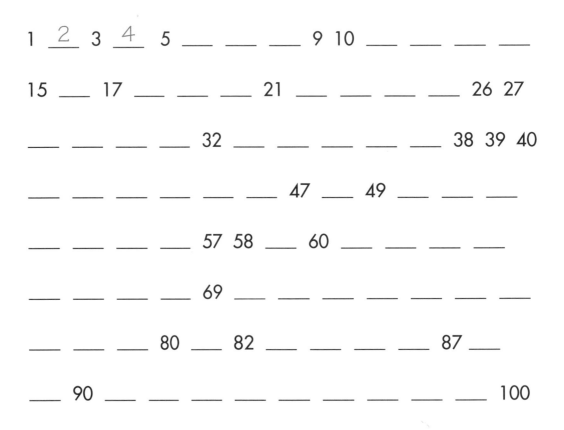

1 _2_ 3 _4_ 5 ___ ___ ___ 9 10 ___ ___ ___ ___

15 ___ 17 ___ ___ ___ 21 ___ ___ ___ ___ 26 27

___ ___ ___ ___ 32 ___ ___ ___ ___ ___ 38 39 40

___ ___ ___ ___ ___ ___ 47 ___ 49 ___ ___ ___

___ ___ ___ ___ 57 58 ___ 60 ___ ___ ___ ___

___ ___ ___ ___ 69 ___ ___ ___ ___ ___ ___ ___

___ ___ ___ 80 ___ 82 ___ ___ ___ ___ 87 ___

___ 90 ___ ___ ___ ___ ___ ___ ___ 100

Number Practice

Count. Then **write** the number.

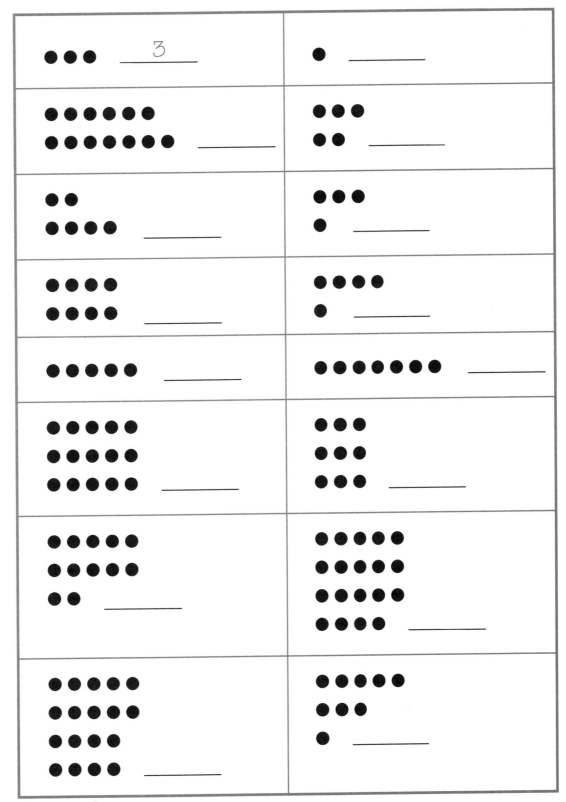

BINGO

Write a number in each box.
Listen to your teacher. **Put** an X on the number you hear.

······· Envelope Practice

A. Look at Adela's envelope.

Adela writes to her mother in El Salvador.

She writes her address here.

Adela Flores
125 West Avenue
Miami, FL 36520
USA

50¢

Rosa López
Calle 24, Apartado 36
La Unión, El Salvador
C.A.

VIA AIR MAIL

She writes her mother's address here.

B. Write your address here.

Name _____

Street _____   Apt. Number

50¢

City   State   Zip _____

Country _____

_____

_____

_____

C. Write the address of your family member here.

Money

Copy

dollar dollar ________ ________ cents ________

$ ________ ________ ¢ ________ ________

	penny	1¢	$.01
	nickel	5¢	$.05
	dime	10¢	$.10
	quarter	25¢	$.25
	dollar	$1.00	
	5 dollars	$5.00	
	10 dollars	$10.00	
	20 dollars	$20.00	

Copy the prices.
Use the money cards to show the prices.

29¢
_____

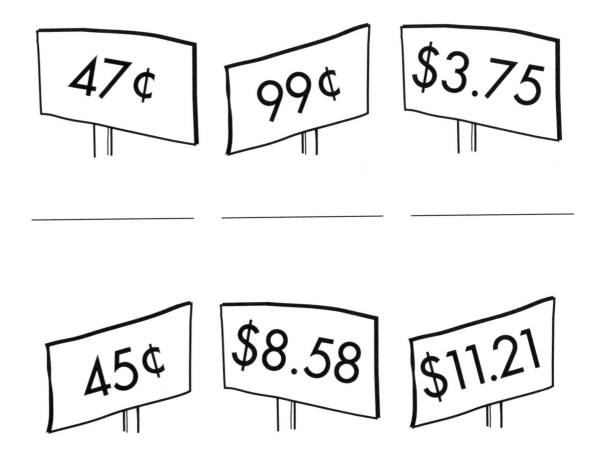

_____   _____   _____

_____   _____   _____

Match

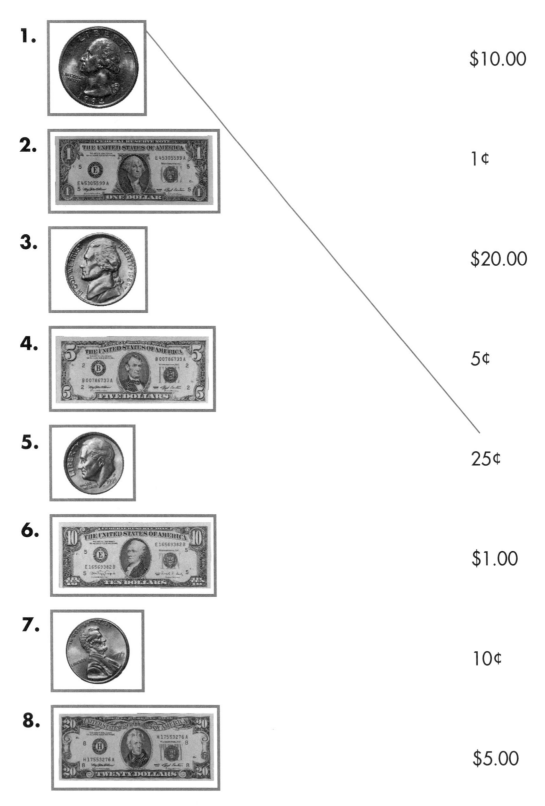

1.

$10.00

2.

1¢

3.

$20.00

4.

5¢

5.

25¢

6.

$1.00

7.

10¢

8.

$5.00

········Clock Practice

Look at the time.
Draw the hands on the clock. **Write** the time.

Clock Practice

Look at the time.

Draw the hands on the clock. **Write** the time.

1:30
1 : 30
7:30
2:30
8:30
3:30
9:30
4:30
10:30
5:30
11:30
6:30
12:30

© 1997 Heinle & Heinle Publishers

Clock Practice

Match the clocks with the same time.

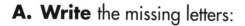

Calendar Practice

A. Write the missing letters:

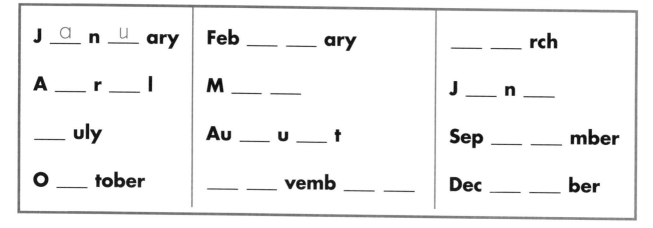

J _a_ n _u_ ary	Feb ___ ___ ary	___ ___ rch
A ___ r ___ l	M ___ ___	J ___ n ___
___ uly	Au ___ u ___ t	Sep ___ ___ mber
O ___ tober	___ ___ vemb ___ ___	Dec ___ ___ ber

B. Match the months, numbers, and abbreviations.

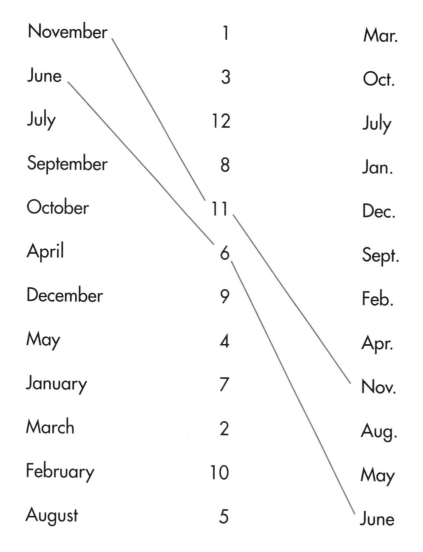

November	1	Mar.
June	3	Oct.
July	12	July
September	8	Jan.
October	11	Dec.
April	6	Sept.
December	9	Feb.
May	4	Apr.
January	7	Nov.
March	2	Aug.
February	10	May
August	5	June

© 1997 Heinle & Heinle Publishers

136 •••

······ Calendar Practice

1 January	**2** February	**3** March
4 April	**5** May	**6** June
7 July	**8** August	**9** September
10 October	**11** November	**12** December

A. Unscramble the words.
Write the words.

beFruray   *February* _____

ugstuA _____

lyJu _____

chaMr _____

emNovbre _____

uryaJan _____

pAril _____

emSepbert _____

aMy _____

beremDec _____

enJu _____

oOctbre _____

.... Calendar and Date Practice

January	Jan.	February	Feb.	March	Mar.
April	Apr.	May	May	June	June
July	July	August	Aug.	September	Sept.
October	Oct.	November	Nov.	December	Dec.

A. Look at the three ways to write the date.
Copy the dates.

October 12, 1996   Oct. 12, 1996   10/12/96

_____   _____   _____

B. What is your birthdate?
Write your birthdate three ways.

1. _____

2. _____

3. _____

C. Practice saying your birthdate three ways.

D. Write today's date three ways.

1. _____

2. _____

3. _____

E. Practice saying the date three ways.

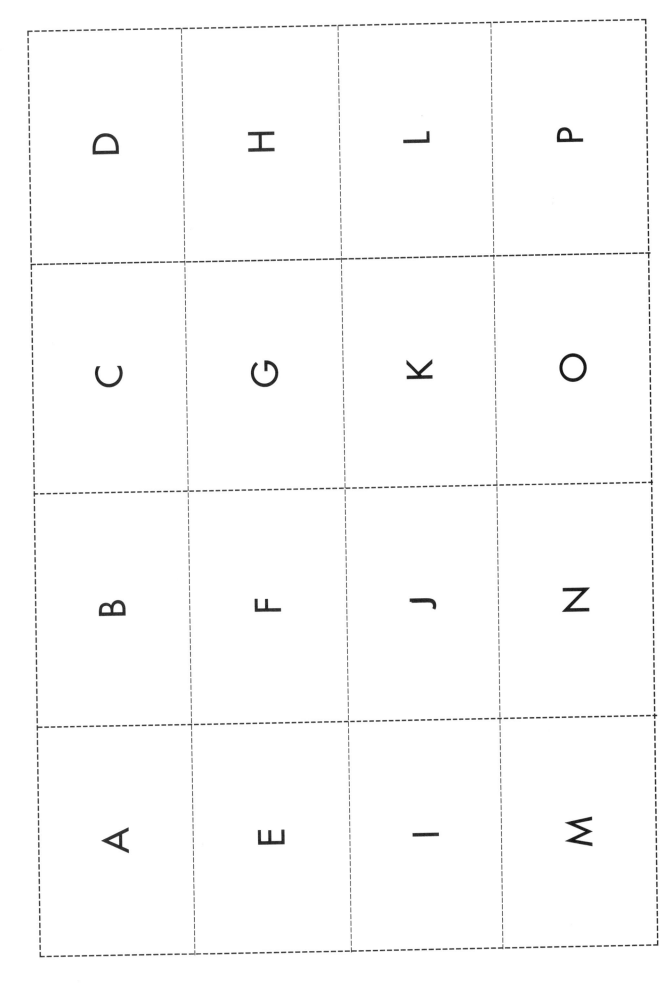

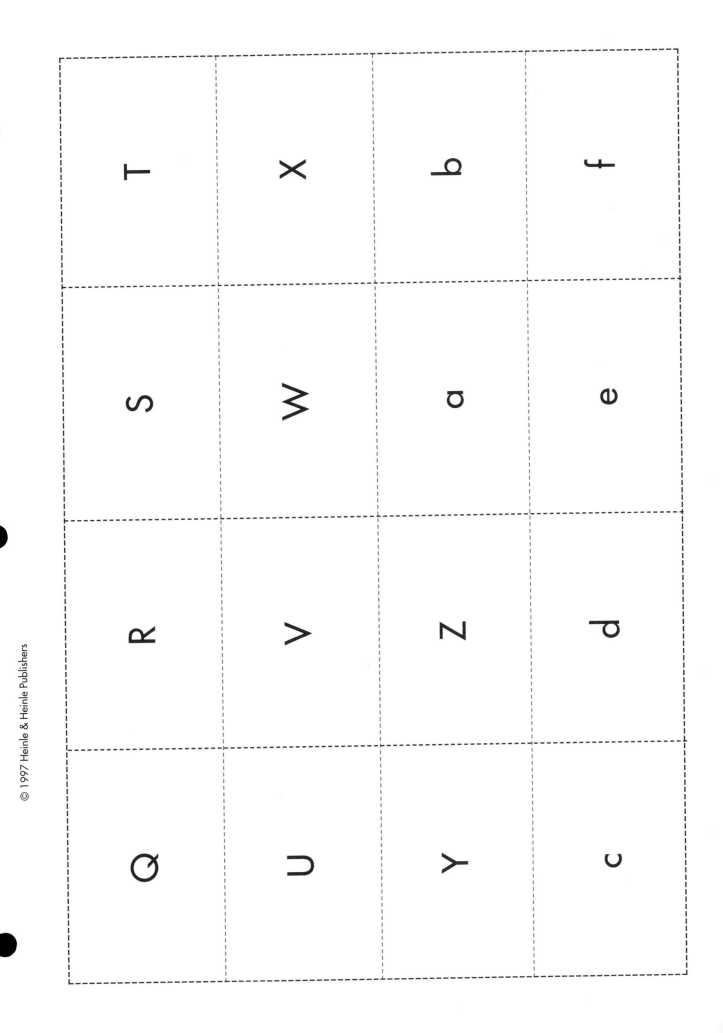

Q	R	S	T
U	V	W	X
Y	Z	a	b
c	d	e	f

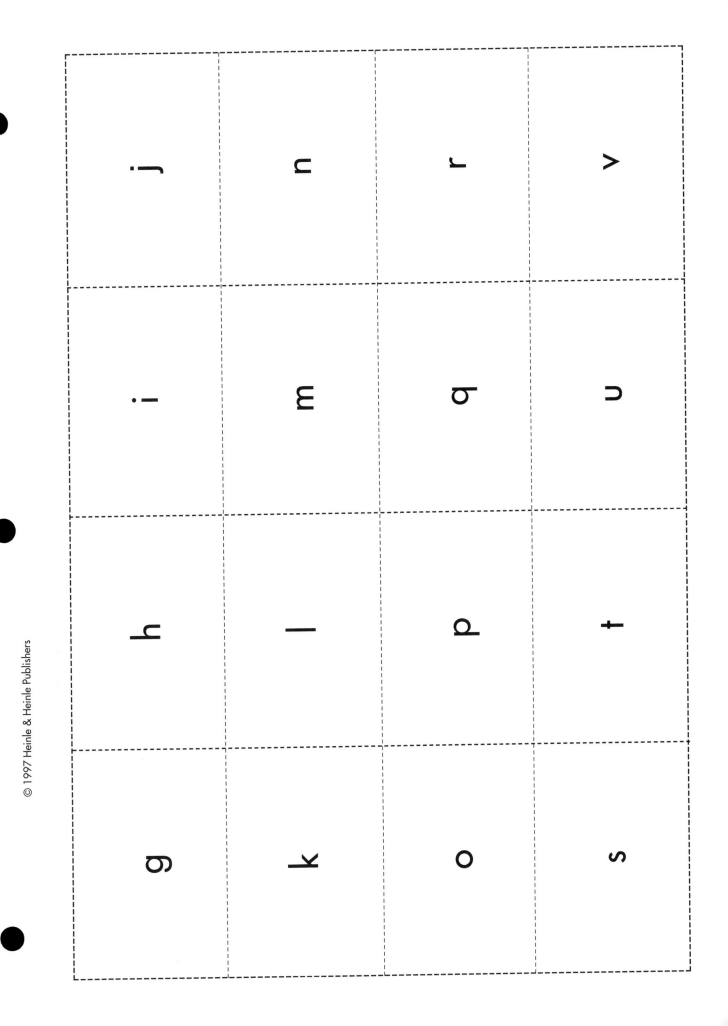

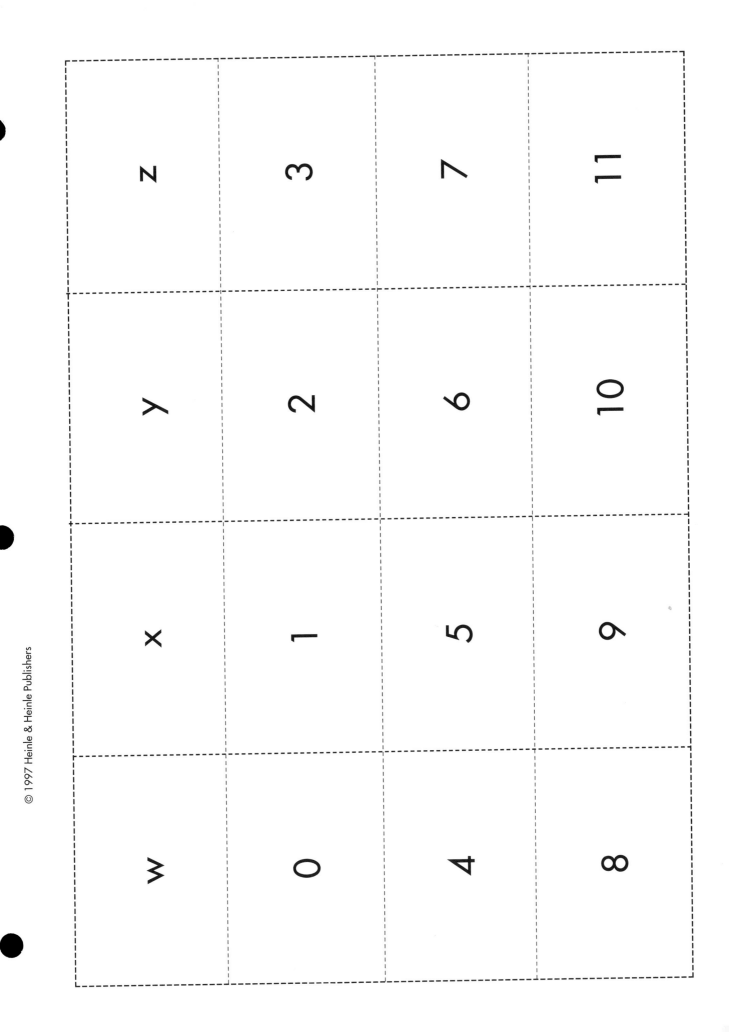

15	14	13	12
19	18	17	16
50	40	30	20
90	80	70	60

Clock

A. Write the missing numbers on the clock.
   Cut out the clock hands.
   Pin the hands to the clock.

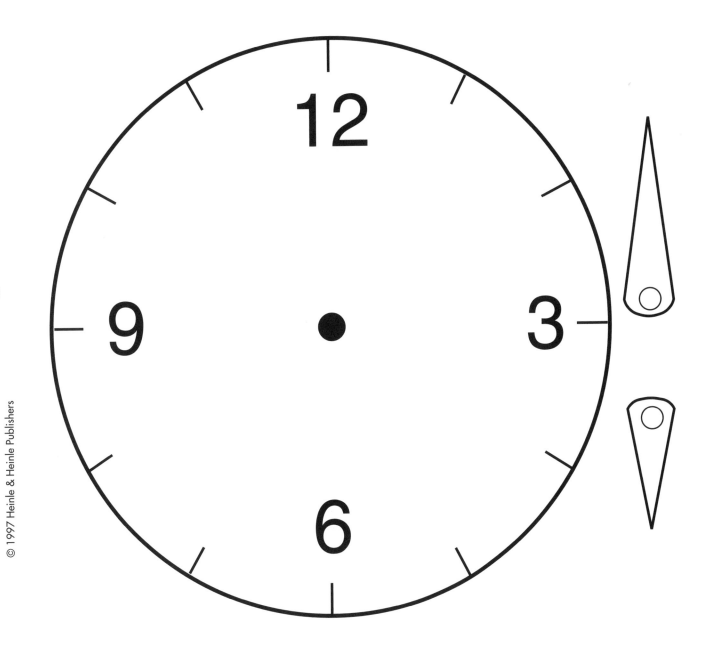

B. Listen to the time. **Move** the hands on the clock.

Calendar

Calendar Cards

A. Cut out the days of the week and abbreviations. **Mix** the cards. **Match** them.

S	M	T	W	T	F	S
Sunday	Monday	Tuesday	Wednesday	Thursday	Friday	Saturday
Sun.	Mon.	Tues.	Wed.	Thurs.	Fri.	Sat.

B. Cut out the number cards. **Make** a calendar for this month. **Put** the days and numbers on the blank calendar.

1	2	3	4	5	6	7
8	9	10	11	12	13	14
15	16	17	18	19	20	21
22	23	24	25	26	27	28
29	30	31				

······ Money

Cut out the money.

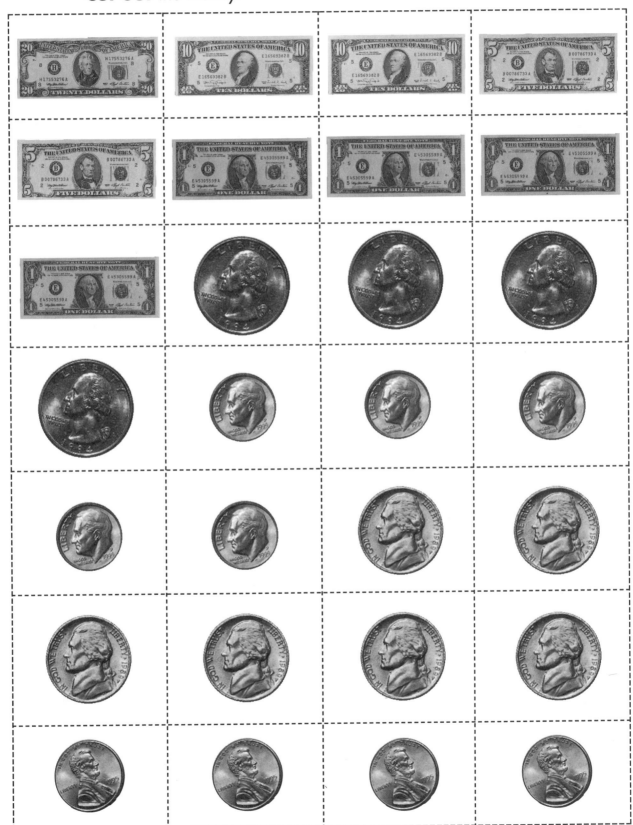